400   6/14 '56

Ann Ford

The Lady was a Skipper

The Lady was a

The story of ELEANOR WILSON,

missionary extraordinary, to the Marshall and Caroline Islands,

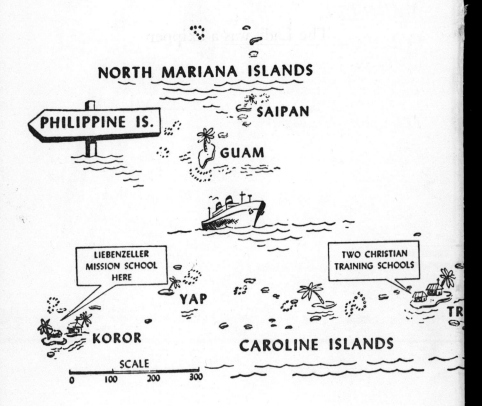

Skipper

by
MARIBELLE
CORMACK

Foreword by
ELEANOR WILSON

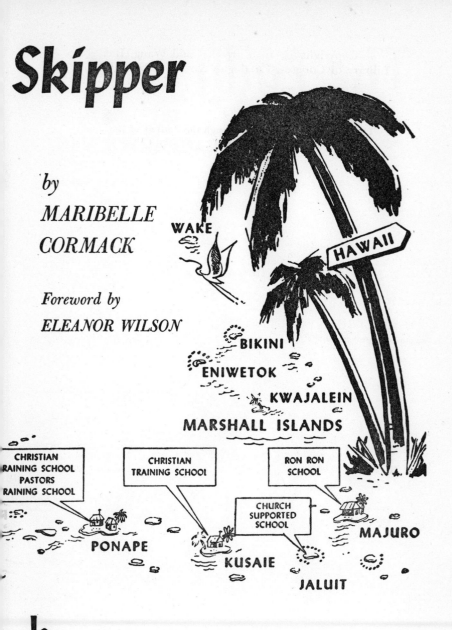

WAKE

HAWAII

BIKINI

ENIWETOK

KWAJALEIN

MARSHALL ISLANDS

CHRISTIAN
RAINING SCHOOL
PASTORS
RAINING SCHOOL

CHRISTIAN
TRAINING SCHOOL

RON RON
SCHOOL

CHURCH
SUPPORTED
SCHOOL

MAJURO

PONAPE

KUSAIE

JALUIT

Hill and Wang, Inc. · New York · 1956

Manufactured in the United States of America
American Book–Stratford Press, Inc., New York

Contents

Contents

Introduction

IT WAS IN 1936 that I first saw the magnificent peaks of mountainous Kusaie rising out of the blue ocean. Still I had no forewarning that someday I should sail these seas myself, and scan the horizon for those same peaks to guide my ship to its haven. Instead I wondered what life would be like on Kusaie where I would be utterly cut off from the world outside.

Micronesia is a far cry from Cambridge, Massachusetts, and yet since the late days of the 1700's there have been close ties between these tiny dots in the Pacific and my home state. If, in the heydey of whaling, you had stopped any seafarer on the streets of Boston, New Bedford or Nantucket he could have told you the latitude and longitude of the Marshalls and the Carolines. Many a sea captain from Massachusetts sailed these waters. On the old charts, Ebon, the southernmost island of the Marshalls is marked Boston Island; and Kusaie in the Carolines, Strong's Island, after the Governor of Massachusetts. And there are islanders alive today who trace their ancestry from many an old seaport in New England.

Away back in 1852 the first Congregational missionaries went to Kusaie. In 1857, in their new ship, *Morning Star I,* they went to Ebon in the Marshalls. It was only by a miracle that they were saved from massacre by a native of Ebon whom they had befriended in Kusaie. Since 1857, with one long gap, a *Morning Star* has brought missionaries, Bibles, schoolbooks, and many other good things to the islanders. The mission ship, "God's Little White Ship," is deeply interwoven with island tradition. As a child of twelve, I gave my pennies in Sunday School to help purchase *Morning Star V*. Never in my wildest dreams could I have imagined that I should one day skipper her successor, *Morning Star VI*, in the years of grace 1950 and 1951.

I do not come of seafaring people. So far as I know not a single one of my ancestors was a sea captain before me. I come of a family of scholars. Both my father's and mother's families arrived in New England from Great Britain in the 1600's. I was born in Norwalk, Connecticut on November 3, 1891. I do not remember our home in Connecticut for we moved to Cambridge when I was 3. My father and mother met when both were teachers in the Hartford High School. Later my father owned a boy's preparatory school and my mother conducted a private elementary school in Cambridge. None of the children in our family went to public schools until we were ready for high school.

My father died in 1901 when I was ten. Only one brother had then finished college and my mother ran her own school to enable the rest of us to go to college. She was a remarkable woman and was greatly loved and admired by all her family and friends. Besides teaching, she did all her own housework and was active in the Y.W.C.A. as well as the First Congregational Church of Cambridge, to which we belonged.

I attended Cambridge Latin School. In 1908 when I was 16, I suffered the severest blow of my life when my mother died. Life without her strong and vibrant personality seemed an ordeal scarcely to be faced. I did not go to school for two years but spent one visiting friends in New York and another keeping house for my brother and sister in Cambridge. In 1911 I entered Simmons College and in 1914 looked about for a business position. The thought of entering religious work never once occurred to me. I had been trained for business and was sure that was to be my work. I took a secretarial position.

In 1921 a sense of dissatisfaction came over me. My brothers and sister had entered various professions and were busy with their careers. In this family of professional people, I was the only one who had not found his lifework. I was in my thirtieth year, and what had I done to make the world better? I felt a sense of obligation, a strong compulsion to do something constructive with my life.

At this time I was sharing an apartment with a social welfare worker who urged me to enter her field. I consulted with a minister and his wife, who were very close to me. But it was a Miss Bair, a dear friend of my mother's, who influenced me most. "I covet you for distinctly religious work," she said earnestly.

It came to me that perhaps this was the work for which I was intended. I left my congenial business position and entered the Biblical Seminary in New York. After graduation in 1923 I became Director of General and Religious Education at the Y.W.C.A. in Kalamazoo, Michigan.

Even then, I had no notion of undertaking the arduous life of a foreign missionary. However in 1924, when asked if I would be willing to go to Japan to work with the graduates of the mission girls' high school in Matsuyama, I paused to consider. I did not care to go to the foreign field but, if I had entered the Lord's work with sincerity of purpose, was I to do as I wished or to go where I was needed? After much prayer over the matter I wrote saying that I was not a good language student but, if they felt it wise to send me to Japan, I would conclude that it was the Lord's plan for my life, and I would go.

I left for Japan in August 1925, intrigued with the task for which I was preparing. All the long months at language school, I looked forward to it. I was to be sent to the tiny outlying villages of the Island of Shikoku, to which the graduates of our girls' school had returned. Often they were the only Christians in the village. We wished to hold these girls to their new faith and to have them organize Sunday Schools for the children of their home village. But this was a task which I was not to perform. Before I completed my language studies, I was assigned as teacher and principal of the Kobe Theological Seminary for Women at Kobe, Japan —in Japanese, the Kobe Joshi Shin Gakko. Here young Japanese women were trained for religious and social welfare work. But again that was not to be my lifework. One of the Board Secretaries resigned and I was invited to take her place. I declined for by then I felt strongly that God wanted me somewhere on the foreign field. However, the Board needed a worker immediately and therefore I came home on special furlough to be an acting associate secretary of the Board at Boston.

Between 1933 and 1935 I was in the Board office at 14 Beacon St., Boston. One of my duties was to find a missionary couple, both of whom spoke Japanese, and who would go out to our Mission Training School in Kusaie in the Caroline Islands, islands that were then under Japanese Mandate. Here students from many parts of Micronesia came to study. They came from places that were only names to me—Truk, Ponape, and the various atolls of the Marshalls. This was long before World War II when the Marshall Islands, and Kwajalein in particular, became places of world interest. These island chains were still far beyond the known horizon of most Americans.

These islands had been claimed by Spain, whose ships had touched there at long intervals since the 1500's, until 1885 when Germany seized them. Then in 1899 she bought the Carolines. In 1914, Japan, as an ally of the U.S.A., moved in and seized both groups. Later in 1919 she secured a mandate over them. From then on, most strangers were unwelcome; however, the missionaries of the American Board of Missions were permitted to carry on their work in the islands. We did not guess in the 1930's that our own flag would, in the next decade, fly over both the Marshalls and the Carolines. Perhaps few Americans except Pacific anthropologists and those who followed the work of the American Board of Missions ever gave the islands a passing thought.

At last I found a missionary in Japan who was willing to go to Kusaie, but his wife did not enjoy the thought of going to so remote a place where there would be no other American woman. I heard the accusing voice of my New England conscience. How could I ask her to go where I was unwilling to go myself? The depression had cut heavily into the Board's resources and there was not enough money to send another missionary. I found that the fare by Japanese freighter was within my means. Careful inquiry lead me to believe that I could live for one year on Kusaie for $150. I decided to go. So with my ticket and this sum of money, I set off by Japanese freighter from Boston to Yokohama where I could catch a smaller Japanese boat, the only transportation to Kusaie in these Japanese Mandated Islands.

As we neared the harbor of Lelu and I had my first glimpse of mountainous Kusaie, my mind was filled with the beauty of the place. I had read that Lelu Harbor was called the Pearl of the Pacific. It certainly shone like a gem set in the sea. The outrigger canoes did not wait for our ship to be anchored but came out to be ready for the eager passengers to jump aboard the moment the "all clear" was given.

We were welcomed by the island pastor, Fred Skillings. Here I realized that even in recent years the islands had ties with New England, for the pastor's father came from Portland, Maine. His sister Hattie married John Sigra, who had become the last king of the island. Fred had married the king's sister. These two interrelated families were the bulwarks of the church. They were to become my close and dear friends. King John and Pastor Skillings came aboard ship wearing white suits with high collars fastened under their chins in the fashion of Japanese officials. We were invited to dinner that evening at the home of the Misses Elizabeth and Jane Baldwin, retired missionaries from New Jersey, who so loved Kusaie that even on their retirement had no thought of going home. They had been more than twenty-four years on Kusaie without once leaving it, even for a short trip to neighboring islands. Dinner was served on their narrow porch as nine persons could not be seated in their small living-dining room. As the meal progressed, I marveled how two Victorian ladies had ever adjusted themselves so perfectly to the life of this tropical island. They seemed as much at home as King John and Queen Hattie, or the pastor and his island wife.

The food was very strange to me. Breadfruit, taro instead of potatoes, and two puddings were served with the main course. These were banana fafa and taro fafa, specialties prepared by the king's own hands. The chicken had been baked on hot stones and, to the foreign palate, it had a peculiar taste. The fried fish *was* delicious and tasted like food prepared at home. As the meal ended, I saw a little cavalcade coming down the white coral road. It was the village band and its members were proudly bearing their instruments. They stopped by the steps of the Baldwins' house and struck up a familiar tune. It was "Home Sweet Home"! Did they intend that I should feel at home on Kusaie or did they want me to realize they were sympathizing with me, because I was so far away from my home in America? I could not look into the future and see that one day Kusaie, perhaps the most beautiful island in the whole world, would be home to me on this side of the earth; that one day I would miss it as I now missed the clipped green lawns of Cambridge and the familiar if noisy sound of trolley cars rolling down Massachusetts Avenue.

The Mission Training School was not at the seaport of Lelu, but on the other side of the mountains and was reached by a waterway through mangrove swamps, and from the water's edge by a steep mountain trail. Here there had been a Congregational School since 1871. I was still officially connected with the Japanese Mission but I soon sent in my resignation. I put down my roots once and for all in Micronesia, first in Kusaie, later in the Marshalls. I think I knew almost from the first that here I had found my lifework.

We had cows, pigs, and chickens at the school, and coconuts and breadfruit grew on the school land. The students studied in the mornings and worked at their tasks in the afternoons. We set out a plantation of pineapples that grow readily in the soil of that high island. My $150 lasted me all through the year. Later, money gifts from friends supplied my needs until Park Street Church at the famous old "Brimstone Corner" in Boston offered to support me as its missionary.

In 1939, Miss Elizabeth Baldwin died. Miss Jane was left quite desolate. By 1940 we in the islands sensed that war might come. Miss Jane had hoped to die in Kusaie and be buried beside her sister. But she was in her seventies and her sight was failing. She had lived in Kusaie through the First World War when the Japanese had come to supplant the Germans. The thought of living there through another war daunted even her hardy spirit. Now she wished to go home to New Jersey. It was quite impossible for her to go alone and I agreed to take her. We were fortunate for, had we stayed, we should have suffered internment under the Japanese. The school was left in charge of a Japanese Christian worker and a very able young Marshallese teacher, Isaac Lanwi, one day to become a famous oculist in the Islands.

Upon my return I kept house for my brother Theodore in Maryland. Then in 1944, the Board sent me up and down the east coast and as far west as Minnesota to tell the American people about the Marshall Islands, then very much in the news, and about Truk, Ponape and Kusaie in the Carolines. With an aching heart, I read of the bombings and of the storming of Kwajalein. What would this mean to our island Christians? Could their faith endure invasion by a people whom they had long thought of as their brothers in Christ?

In December 1945, I left Boston for Hawaii. In February 1946, in the famous Kawaihao Church there, I was ordained as a Christian minister, that I might better serve the islands on my return. It was August 1946 when I finally received permission to fly from Hawaii to the Marshall Islands.

My welcome back to these islands is told in this book. I say "back" though actually I had been in the Marshalls only twice before the war. However, many of the Marshallese people had attended our school at Kusaie and therefore I went to them as a friend and not as a stranger.

Conditions in the widely scattered, low atolls of the Marshalls were quite different than in the close-knit islands that form the Kusaien group. In Kusaie we could go anywhere among the eight islands by canoe on sheltered inland waterways. In the Marshalls we were helpless to visit the churches of the other atolls without a fair-sized boat. In Japanese days the students could travel to Kusaie by Japanese freighters which serviced the islands on regular schedules. Now there were no commercial ships.

We made our appeal to the Board for a ship, and in 1948, *Morning Star VI,* a schooner with auxiliary power, came out to us. She had once been the yacht, *Norseman,* of Boston. She received in Kusaie a welcome such as only the islanders can give. Again a tradition had been effectively upheld— God's Little White Ship would again link the island missions together. I was in Kusaie when she arrived. I have never known quite such an uplifting of the heart as I felt when I saw her white sails and her blue mission pennant with its white dove. She made Boston seem very near!

It was in March 1950 that I became her skipper. There was no other American Board missionary in the Marshalls at that time, so this task fell to my unprepared hands. I studied navigation, learned to trust my native crew for seamanship, and while I was master of her, by God's grace, we suffered no accident. My skippering the *Star* was chosen as the theme of this book because that was the most unusual experience of all my years as foreign missionary.

I had been asked many times to write my biography but I had neither the time nor the writing experience. It was in August 1953, off my own island of Kusaie, that I met the future author of this book. Miss Cormack was touring the islands for background material to rebuild Pacific Hall in the Park Museum at Providence, R.I., and for her current novel whose scene is laid in these waters. I had chaperoned a group of students from the Marshalls to Kusaie, not knowing how I would get back. However, the day after my arrival an unexpected government ship, the motor vessel *Gunner's Knot,* lay off the island to discharge Kusaien passengers. That was my chance to return to the Marshalls.

When I stepped from the ladder to the deck I was surprised to be greeted by an American woman. "Are you a teacher or a nurse?" she asked. "I am a missionary," I answered. So we two New England spinsters, whose homes were barely fifty miles apart, met like two old-time whaling masters "on the line."

It did not strike me till long afterwards, when I read Miss Cormack's sprightly letters, that in her I had found the author for my book. Our meeting seemed something more than coincidence. She was a writer with a shelf of books to her credit; she had spent three years studying the anthropology of the islands; she was an ardent lover of the sea and was herself a navigator. She had visited or touched at all the island groups where I had worked. In the Marshalls she saw me with my parishioners. And moreover she had the strong Biblical background that gave meaning to my work.

I sent her what she ruefully described as "a cubic yard of notes." She studied the history of the mission work in the islands; of all the former *Morning Stars.* Indeed, she had already heard of *Morning Star I,* on a radio program, to which she had tuned quite by chance. She told me how the story had delighted her. This was long before she had any prospects of visiting these islands, for hers was a one-girl expedition financed entirely by herself. I believe she was the first civilian not on a government or scientific assignment to make the entire circuit of the Micronesian Islands, since the close of World War II.

I wish I could tell you that *Morning Star VI* still sails these waters just above the equator but that would not be true. My ship fell on evil days while I was home in 1951 on leave. Then a fine and devoted captain was found in Creston Ketchum of Canada, but, by the time he took over, the ship was in grave need of repairs, unobtainable in the islands. He skippered her safely for six months when she was pronounced unfit. She was being towed from Ponape to the Marshalls when a bad storm battered her weakened hull and broke her towline. The pumps could not save her. Aboard her, Captain Ketchum, and Antolin, his crewman, knew she was doomed. It was impossible to launch a boat. There was nothing to do but swim to the *Torry* which was standing by. Ketchum and Antolin leaped into the sea where sharks are the oldest inhabitants. Antolin climbed aboard by the aid of a dangling rope, but Ketchum was too weak to try. Then a wave lifted him on its crest and swept him level with the deck of the *Torry*. The chief mate reached out and dragged him aboard. Still another tradition was preserved. Not a single life was ever lost aboard a *Morning Star* while the ship flew the Mission pennant. Ships had been lost but never a crewman's life.

Since I returned to the islands in 1952, I have been seriously hampered for lack of a ship. To reach the scattered churches of my parish I have had to thumb rides on copra boats and all sorts of craft. Sometimes Marshallese pastors have been unable to get to their biennial meetings. Many of the older workers cannot read English and need the refresher courses given at those conferences. Sometimes there is no government boat. Sometimes there is no room aboard one. The need for *Morning Star VII* is great.

My hitchhiking to Kusaie and back was more successful than some of my trips. Because of the lack of a ship of our own, I nearly missed being home for Christmas in 1955. My leave had come but the little island steamer changed its schedule and I wondered if I would arrive in Cambridge for the holidays. It was with a grateful heart that I boarded a fifty-foot copra boat which put in at Jabwor on its way to Kwajalein. It should have been an easy trip, straight northwest up the western chain of the islands, a route well known both to the captain and myself.

But his crew, like my own on the *Morning Star,* changed compass course in the night without recording it and next morning we saw no sign of Ailinglaplap, the halfway marker on our journey. We had no radio and no sextant. The island captain navigated by wave patterns, but this time they all seemed to vanish into sea, rather than guide us to land. Instead of our comforting chain of marker islands, all that day we saw nothing but empty sea. We did not reach our destination that night as expected. We had no way of knowing where we were. At last the captain asked me which way I would go. I hesitated. He thought we had been west of Ailinglaplap but I felt we had always been east of that atoll.

"I would go due west for three or four hours," I said, "and then head to the northwest. I cannot justify my feeling, but I believe that is the right course."

Our fuel was getting low. If we got west of Kwajalein, it would be almost impossible to beat back against the prevailing east winds and the captain had only jib and fores'le—no main's'le at all. After considering the situation, the captain called "Riuk" and we came about so as to head northwest. The following day we were sighted by the *Sussex,* a navy supply ship, four days ahead of schedule. I was invited aboard and the captain showed me his chart. We were seventy miles mostly east and slightly north of our destination. My guess had been right. I ceased to wonder how my Marshallese crew felt their way over these seas. Even I—a landlubber, an outlander, a student of books—had developed in just eighteen months something of this sea sense.

At Kwajalein I caught a plane for Honolulu, at Honolulu another for the States and thus I arrived home in Cambridge on Christmas Eve. My family was waiting for me, a reunion long planned. I had achieved the fondest wish of the far-traveler, of the deep seafarer—I was home with my dear ones for Christmas!

As this book goes to press in the spring of 1956, I am

about to return to my mission at Jabwor, Jaluit Atoll. It is my hope that this story may bring closer to the hearts and minds of Americans, the Islands of The Trust Territory of the Pacific, U.S.A.

ELEANOR WILSON

Cambridge, Massachusetts
April, 1956

CHAPTER I

Paper Jack Skipper

ELEANOR WILSON sat by the rail of her first command, *Morning Star VI,* riding secure in the vast roadstead of Kwajalein. The trim white schooner rode the waves like a sea bird that had settled on the water after a long flight over the sea. Beside the giant albatross of a Navy tanker anchored a quarter of a mile away, the *Star* seemed like a tiny sea bird. She strained at her anchors, as if anxious to be about her proper business among these reefs and atolls. Both the *Star* and its mistress belonged in this world of coconut palms, of sandy atolls and treacherous green water that marked the presence of coral reefs, reefs that could slice through the *Star's* wooden hull.

Kwajalein was still a great naval base in the mid-Pacific. A few years before, vast armadas of the United States Fleet had assembled here, and from here were staged the amphibious invasions that paved the way for victory in World War II. There was anchorage space in this lagoon for our entire invasion force. The *Star,* a single tanker, a few LST's, and a flying boat looked lonely now on the wide expanse of water. For this was March, 1950, and peace had come to these islands five years before. Sand had almost filled in the bomb craters and new coconut palms were growing to replace those that had been destroyed.

A white tern settled on the masthead of the schooner, poised there a moment and preened its wing. There were so few birds in the Marshall Islands, except on remote and uninhabited "bird islands," that at sea the presence of a single

one of a certain species gave the island navigator a clue to
the direction and the distance of the nearest land. The tern
looked down appraisingly at the white ship and the white-
haired lady in the white dress, as if questioning their right
to be here. The lagoon at Kwajalein might at first glance
seem an unlikely setting for two New Englanders—Miss
Eleanor Wilson, whose home was close by Harvard Yard,
and the schooner, once the yacht *Norseman,* of Boston. Yet
the lady was no stranger here. She was an old resident of
Micronesia. Only the yacht was a relative newcomer—until
this tour of duty its bowsprit had been thrust only into the
well-charted seas between Nantucket and Casco Bay, seas
patrolled by a vigilant Coast Guard.

But here in the equatorial waters of the Pacific there was
no such protection, no safeguards to make sailing easy. Once
they left the shelter of this lagoon, schooner and lady must
go it alone. There was neither lighthouse nor buoy to guide
them, and the schooner's generator that powered the radio
had long since given up the ghost after repeated dousings in
sea water from the bilge. The engine, for the time at least,
was out of repair, the needed parts being unobtainable in
any Pacific port within call. Even the sails of the once sleek
yacht were mended and worn. They would rip to shreds in
the first tropic gale. The chronometer—that indispensable
timepiece at sea—would not keep accurate time. Without
accurate time, not even an expert navigator could get his
position. And they had no navigator—only a native crew of
Marshallese—and there was doubt if these islanders would
sail with a woman in command. In such circumstances
Eleanor Wilson became Mistress, or Master, of the *Morning
Star*!

She was no seaman. There was not even salt in her veins.
Born a Connecticut Yankee, and reared in Cambridge,
Massachusetts, she came of a family of scholars. She had
never sailed so much as a catboat on a millpond. At sea, she
had always been a passenger, and the "ships" she had known
in her years in these islands were outrigger canoes hollowed

from a single log of a breadfruit tree, or carefully fashioned from breadfruit boards. She was used to danger, to hardship, to being drenched as she went about her sea-borne parish, but she had never had command of a ship. Now she was expected to sail the *Star*, the precious missionary ship, among reefs as dangerous as any in all the world!

As a missionary, she had been asked to marry couples who had waited long for the ceremony, to baptize babies, nurse the sick and teach the young. She had traveled through jungles and across barren islands to preach in many languages, but never this! And she was 58! It was middling late for anyone to grow web feet.

She looked about her at the lagoon and the fringe of low islands that stretched along the reef far to the northwest. Kwajalein is in the Sunset Chain of the Marshall Islands. Her mission at Rong Rong on Majuro Atoll was in the Sunrise Chain, two hundred and forty-three miles to the southeast. The equator lay just south of these islands, the date line only nine degrees to the east. They were in the middle of the earth and the middle of the Pacific Ocean.

Eleanor thought of the fairy tale land that lay east of the sun and west of the moon. Even so, between sun and moon she must sail this ship with only the stars for guides. It was enough to make any heart quail.

The radiogram that had turned a missionary teacher into a ship captain had reached her at Majuro five days before. She took it from her pocket and read it again, as if she could not believe the written words:
"COME TO KWAJALEIN AND TAKE OVER THE *MORNING STAR*"

It was signed by Harold Hanlin. Dr. Hanlin was also a missionary of the American Board of Commissioners for Foreign Missions in these islands, and he had been called home. That left Eleanor Wilson as the only career representative of that old and honorable body in the Marshall Islands. She was, therefore, in full charge of the mission schooner, the *Star*.

Majuro Atoll—almost 250 miles from Kwajalein—had been her headquarters since her return to the islands at the close of World War II. It had been considered unwise to send a lone woman westward to Kusaie in the Carolines. To Eleanor this had seemed downright foolish, for Kusaie was her second home where, under Japanese rule before the war, she had been principal of the Congregational Mission School. King and commoner were her fellow Christians and devoted friends, for the Congregational Mission at Kusaie had been established in 1852. However, she had bowed to Navy regulations and begun a new school here at Rong Rong close by the Coast Guard Station, just twenty miles up the lagoon from Uliga, administrative headquarters of the Navy in the Marshall Islands.

Her one-room house served also as her office at Rong Rong Mission on the northern tip of Majuro Atoll. She had been mimeographing the Sunday School lessons for her twenty-eight island churches, when the silence was broken by the crunching of boots on the coral path. That could mean only an American. The bare brown feet of the Marshallese made no such sound on the well-worn path, so it was not one of her students or parishioners. It must be one of the young men from the Coast Guard Station. There were no other strangers near the mission school.

"Hi, Miss Wilson," a cheery young voice called. "Got a message for you. It just came in." He grinned at her and saluted in a manner half teasing, half serious. "Guess I'll have to call you Captain now, ma'am. You just got yourself a ship!" There was something close to envy in his tone. He had joined the Coast Guard to go to sea, and here he was playing telegraph boy on a strip of coral!

Eleanor read the message. "Oh, it's a mistake," she said. "They couldn't expect me to sail the *Star*! I was just to look after her here at Rong Rong Mission. Dr. Hanlin was to sail her here before he left." Her words convinced neither of them, certainly not herself, but she went on desperately, struggling against the suspicion of what lay ahead. "I was just to see that the crew washed down her decks and kept the brass shined. I'm no sailor. I was so seasick my first trip aboard her, I never wanted to set foot on her again." Her eyes met those of the young coast guardsman. They regarded each other steadily for a long moment.

"Ma'am," he said, as if he were addressing a fellow member of the armed forces, "that may all be true, but that radiogram sounds mighty like orders to me. It says to come to Kwaj and take over the *Star*. Couldn't be plainer. You'd better get ready, ma'am. This is Wednesday and the next plane from Uliga is on Sunday. We can take you down in the launch Sunday morning."

"Thanks! It's a long, hot trip by canoe, and I hate to arrive pickled in brine!"

She looked about her one-room house, built of old lumber salvaged from Navy installations. She looked with regret at her "picture" window, a yard-square piece of glass with only one crack in it, diagonally. The crack bisected the view of coral beach and blue water, but the window framed a pandanus tree beautifully, from luscious fruit and drooping fronds of foliage to the arched roots exposed above the scant soil of the atoll. This was home now, her second home in the Marshalls. This was the place she had built when she came to Rong Rong to found a new school. There in the corner was the old, rusted mimeograph, indispensable tool of her profession. She thought of the food in the kerosene refrigerator. Well, it would not go to waste. The other teachers could use it. She could leave many tasks to them, but she must finish these lesson sheets. The old mimeograph clicked as page after page flew from the roller. Then she made a list of what must be done before she left.

Plainly someone else would have to take her classes. She had no time to teach school. There was a sermon which must be written for Sunday morning. That, no one could do for her. And she must have something to wear on the boat. Well, the island girls were good seamstresses. Luckily she had on hand a dress length of white cotton cloth. Paper patterns were unknown, but the girls did well enough without them. Besides, this was for the waters of the Marshall Islands, not those of Long Island Sound. They had three days! With hand-powered machines, they would need them.

What a lot must be done before she could leave on Sunday to make that plane! She knew that her work would be interrupted by well-wishers who would come to call, and never was a call made in the Marshall Islands without the sharing of food. It was as rigid a ceremonial as the cup of tea offered to every visitor to cot or castle in ancient Scotland.

Somehow by Sunday everything was done. Her sailing costume was packed in her single bag. How would she manage in the narrow quarters of a tossing ship, the only woman in a world of men? She stood a moment and listened to the beating of the surf on the beach and the sound of the wind whipping the branches of the pandanus tree.

She was used to sudden orders and to traveling light. Seven years in Japan and nine in these island chains had made the unexpected the usual order of the day. Yet her single suitcase did seem a trifle inadequate. Eleanor felt that this bag should be a sea chest and that she should be shouldering it to walk down the jetty to a sailing ship with tall masts gleaming in the sunlight. That was the way it was pictured in the sea tales when a young man made his start at the most exacting of all careers.

But there was no jetty at the mission, only the shore of coral sand and a few straggling coconuts along the water's edge. She took the lagoon path to the Coast Guard pier, feeling rather like a feminine Pied Piper as all the teachers and pupils of her school fell in behind. She stepped aboard the waiting launch.

"Yokwe Kom!" she called back to the group on the shore.

"Yokwe Yuk!" they answered.

It was the universal island greeting. It was the "Aloha" of the Marshalls. There was no sorrow in this parting. They were sure she would return.

The launch headed down the lagoon. The sea was relatively calm inside the reef. Eleanor glanced over her shoulder to windward. She had been too long in the islands not to note the wind direction many times a day. Here at Rong Rong on the tip of Majuro Atoll they lived intimately with wind and wave, the highest land rising no more than six feet above high tide mark. Luckily they were not in the hurricane belt, but if a tidal wave should ever hit them, there was no doubt where they would go.

Indeed, here in the islands where life clung tenuously to a strip of sand, one seemed almost to touch the outer fringes of eternity. Perhaps, Eleanor thought, this accounted in some measure for the piety of the islanders. Often their devotion made even their missionary wonder. They lived so close to the borderland between life and death that they were nearer than any mainlander to the eternal verities.

Sharks, waves, and currents! These were all things that Eleanor must reckon with if she were to command the *Star!* The islanders were master seamen. With them seamanship was instinctive, an inherited skill developed over centuries. This she knew. Put one adrift on a log and he would somehow head for the nearest land. Their old-time navigators knew the course from island to island by wave pattern, by flight of birds, by the presence of certain fishes, by the stars; but the old skills in making long voyages had been largely forgotten and few young Marshallese today knew more than how to sail by familiar landmarks to some nearby island. Many had never left their own atoll. Inside the reef, dangers were few, especially to men who swam like otter, but one of these dangers was not easily forgotten—the ever-present threat of sharks. Fishing was not as dangerous as in northern waters, for the islander was not a deep-sea fisherman. His best fishing ground was the reef, particularly in the shelter of the lagoon, yet even here there were treacherous waves and currents for which he must allow. No equatorial waters were free from sharks. The blood of a speared fish might bring these monsters swarming about his canoe.

The journey from Rong Rong to Kwajalein had sorely tried her patience. Patience was a virtue, and one learned best in tribulation, but the delay in getting here had been maddening when haste was so imperative. They had made good time to Uliga. There had been a Navy jeep waiting on the pier—for someone else. Yet the driver had driven like mad to the airstrip in the hope of getting her to the plane, and they had missed it by scarcely a minute! It was just taking off from the runway. Eleanor could have wept with weariness and disappointment as the great black plane climbed into the air and headed northwest for Kwajalein— without her. So there had been nothing to do but wait for the plane that would leave on the morrow. She had shrugged in resignation. Something of oriental fatalism clung to her from her missionary years in Japan. Often she wondered if she had taught her students when she was principal of the Kobe Women's Evangelical School or if they had taught her. Life was a school, her father—himself a school principal— had told her, and as long as one lived, one went to it. There was nothing to do but wait for Monday's plane.

It had been mid-afternoon on Monday when they reached Kwajalein. From the beach she had seen the *Star* at anchor. She tried to whistle, but her feeble attempt would not have roused a crab crawling along the beach at her feet. A big Marine, high on the lookout tower overhead, grinned down at her, thrust two fingers in his mouth and emitted an ear-splitting whistle. This, with his gesture, brought the dinghy from the *Morning Star* ashore for her. The lagoon was choppy now, whipped by a northwest wind. The men had to bend their backs to bring the boat into the schooner's lee. From the dinghy it was only a high step to the deck. Eleanor seized the rigging and climbed aboard. Luckabudge, a crewman, was waiting to help her.

"Where is Dr. Hanlin?" she asked in surprise.

Luckabudge stared at her. She didn't know!

Fear gripped Eleanor's heart. Luckabudge looked rueful. "He has finished his going," he said solemnly. Then, searching for the right words in English, he added pains-takingly, "At nine o'clock."

Eleanor felt her knees buckling. She must not show con-sternation—not before the crew. Anliri, the island sailing master, was looking at her questioningly. The three other crewmen were gathered by the mast, waiting for her to speak to them. She did so, calling each one by name.

"Dr. Hanlin . . . couldn't wait even one day for me?" she asked of Luckabudge, who, though not captain, seemed to be the spokesman. Luckabudge shook his head. A sensitive person, he knew what a blow this was to her.

"Navy ship took Dr. Hanlin to Kusaie. His family—in America—very sick," he explained apologetically. Then his face brightened as if he had some good news. "He left you a letter."

Luckabudge ran for the ladder and was back in a moment with a folded piece of paper. The respect of the islander for the written word was tremendous.

Eleanor took the paper. With only this for a guide, she had been left in command! Nor was the note much help. It was merely a list of disastrous facts:

The *Star's* engine had broken down and could not be re-paired until needed parts came out from the States. The sails were nearly past use. New ones had been ordered from Honolulu, but the date of arrival was unpredictable. The electric generator was out of commission, so they were with-out light or power. She would have to get kerosene running lights to comply with the law. The chronometer went steady by jerks and was, therefore, useless for navigation.

For a moment she stood perfectly still, almost stunned. She recalled the words of the young coast guardsman, "Guess I'll have to call you Captain now, ma'am. You just got your-self a ship!"

CHAPTER II

Under Way

So SHE WAS aboard her first command! She knew how a new sea captain must feel on the bridge of his first ship when the pilot has gone over the rail and he is left in sole command. But he would be young and able and trained for his job however arduous it might be. He would *not* be a lady missionary, aged 58, with no pilot whatsoever but the unknown stars overhead. She knew the North Star, but, so close to the equator, it was often hidden in the great banks of cumulous clouds that girdled the horizon. She knew Orion, the Southern Cross, the Seven Sisters, the Big Dipper and the right triangle formed by Vega, Altair and Deneb. That was the extent of her astronomical knowledge. Of navigation, she knew nothing.

The task assigned her was plainly impossible. Had they taken leave of their senses back there in Boston? Were there no capable sea captains available to pilot the *Star* about the mission stations of Micronesia? There were twenty-eight of them here in the Marshalls alone. She might, with the island seamanship of her crew, conceivably cover the Marshalls. But her parish in the Pacific included the Carolines as far west as Truk, which was some thousand miles from Kwajalein. It was a parish of thousands of square miles of ocean, set at wide intervals with tiny groups of islands. Eleanor Wilson felt in this hour rather like a microscopic organism herself, under the glass of the Congregational Church. Even the *Star* was only a dot on this wide ocean. The land area of this parish was less than half that of Rhode Island, a state that had often been referred to in neighboring Massachusetts as merely a "state of mind." Why, all of Micronesia had very little more land than this, scattered like wind-blown grains of sand, coral and earth over a piece of ocean comparable in size to the whole United States! And, ideally, whoever was Master of the *Star,* the one American Board missionary ship in these island chains, ought to be able to sail her across and around them and make a pin-point landing on any dot within the perimeter. Eleanor's head swam.

If she did not do it, then the work would be hindered. At least the link between the churches would be broken. The people would carry on; their faith was strong. But who would bring the new Bibles and hymnbooks, the schoolbooks and supplies to the outlying islets? The Navy did everything it could, but Navy ships could not touch regularly at every distant atoll in her huge parish. The only other transportation was by copra boats which occasionally touched at the various atolls. They had no set schedules and catching one was a mere matter of good luck. Distances from atoll to atoll were too great to travel by canoe.

She took it a step at a time. The *Star* must make its rounds. Since 1857 a *Morning Star* had served this world of islands, with only one long gap. Between 1905 and the outbreak of World War II, German and Japanese commercial steamers had serviced the islands. But still the islanders had remembered the *Star,* their own ship, God's little white ship, its blue pennant with the white dove flying at its masthead.

How great their joy had been when, in 1948, *Morning Star VI* arrived! It was proof of the love of their brothers of the Christian faith in distant Boston, that fabled place from which their first missionaries had come. Eleanor's taut nerves relaxed. For a moment she gave herself up to reverie.

She had come back to the islands in 1946, after becoming an ordained minister in Hawaii, which had been a Congregational Mission stronghold since 1821. She had arrived here at Kwajalein by Navy plane on the twelfth of August. She had celebrated the first anniversary of V-J Day in the islands. Dr. Hanlin, then a Navy chaplain, was stationed here. It was a true homecoming. And how the people of Carlos Island on Kwajalein Atoll had welcomed them! Her eyes grew moist. There was no doubt. They had wanted their missionaries back.

That had startled the Navy authorities. When, after terrible bombings from the air and bombardment from the sea, Kwajalein was taken and the American flag was raised, the people of the atoll had crept from their shallow shelters in the bomb craters in the sand to rejoice. One old woman had held out her mildewed Bible for the Marine to see, proof positive that she was a fellow Christian.

"We are Christians from Boston!" she said proudly. "Now can we pray?"

It was a question she was well-advised to ask of a man in uniform. Prayer had been forbidden by a Japanese officer in the war years. To pray then was to court death, for it had been dangerous to show any sympathy to America or her allies. Their aged missionary, Carl Heine, an Australian, converted oddly enough by a Marshallese girl in the days of his youth, had been martyred in 1944 for fear of the help he might give to an invader. His son and daughter-in-law vanished, their fate unknown. His twelve-year-old grandson swam to the next island, where he found refuge.

The old woman looked timidly at the Marine. He was too nonplussed to answer. Then he collected himself and said heartily, "Lady, you go right ahead and pray! I'd like to see anybody try to stop you!"

Tears filled the eyes of the people. More and more of them gathered about the Marine and the flag. Someone started a song. The words were odd to his ears, but the tune was familiar! The Marine wiped the sweat from his forehead, took off his cap and joined in. It was a long time since he had gone to the Baptist Sunday School. Over the sands and the broken trees of the bombed-out island rang the music, sung as only the islanders can sing it, weak at first and then increasing in volume as they gained in assurance:

"Savior, like a shepherd lead us, Much we need thy tender care."

The Marine got away when he could. His face was flushed when he reported back to his commanding officer.

The commanding officer, too, was looking more than a little astonished. He had sent word for the island chiefs to report to him, and within the half-hour they had come. They stood, barefoot, in their tattered clothes, waiting politely for the chief of the new nation to speak. The Marshallese have fine manners. They are, when it is possible, immaculately clean. It is, however, not possible to be too clean when to maintain life in the weeks past they had burrowed in the sandy earth like moles.

Slowly through an interpreter the commanding officer asked, "What can we do for you?"

There was no consultation. They knew! They were ready with their request.

"Send us back our missionaries!"

"I . . . I'll consult my government," the officer said, not daring to meet the eyes of the Marine.

When the delegation was gone, the commanding officer looked out the door of the hastily erected Quonset hut. He saw a barren strip of coral island pockmarked by bombs dropped from American planes. He saw three ragged coconut palms, all that was left of the green fringe that had once bordered the whole island. There was not a native house left standing. All about him was utter desolation. The people must be starving. Food, water and housing must be provided. And they asked first for their missionaries!

"Do you think they'll believe me in Washington?" the commanding officer said, more to himself than to the Marine.

"Sir, please tell them about the old lady who said she was a Christian from Boston. What did she mean by that, sir?"

The commanding officer understood. "The Boston missionaries have been in these islands for nearly a century. They had churches all over the place. Even had their own ship to service the missions. I guess they did a good job. The people seem to remember."

And so through the mysterious channels by which Navy and Government move, word had reached 14 Beacon Street, Boston, the "High Command" of the American Mission Board, that they might send back their missionaries.

Yet Navy authorities had been a little flustered when Eleanor Wilson had come. The intrepid New England spinster was already a legend, an integral part of island tradition. But to their way of thinking Kwajalein in 1946 was hardly a place for a lady.

She had bunked in the barracks with the Army and Navy nurses, biblically known as "Hell's Angels." And no convent had ever been safer, for day and night a Marine mounted guard at its door and made sure that all "angels" were in at 11:00 P.M. and that no males passed beyond the guardian's desk. Eleanor chuckled, remembering the fury of a newspaper woman at being hauled home from a party at this early hour and incarcerated in the women's barracks. This regulation, however, had not troubled Eleanor. She had lived in worse quarters, slept on harder beds, and been less sure of the strong arm of authority within easy call. She slept soundly.

The next morning a Navy plane had taken her to Majuro Atoll and from there a Navy boat had taken her to the native church at Laura, on Majuro Island. The Mission had then no ship of its own; it was like a blind man without his seeing-eye dog. Commercial transportation was not yet established. Permission had to be secured to travel by Navy ship or plane, particularly on ships where there were no accommodations for privacy for a woman. Eleanor was reasonable. She understood the Navy's reluctance to let her move about.

How could she explain to these young officers, new to these islands, which to them were something out of fiction, that to her this was home? She wanted to return to Kusaie in the distant Carolines, but the Navy felt that would be unwise. Ships were too uncertain to send a white woman alone to such a place. Such a place, indeed, Eleanor thought! Kusaie was, in a manner of speaking, an outpost of New England. It had once been called Strong's Island, after Caleb Strong, Governor of Massachusetts in 1800! Her missionary predecessors had come to this island in 1852, when its people were still hostile and remembered the misdeeds of Spanish pirates and Yankee whalers, and had believed the missionaries were of that same ilk. On Kusaie, beloved of everyone who lived there, she had been principal of the long-established mission school. The King of Kusaie regarded her as a member of his own family, and she had lived there with impunity when it was under Japanese rule!

But she had not demurred. She had agreed to work in the Marshalls and had served first at Laura and then at Rong Rong, which means Hole Hole, or the hole in the reef. All the island languages seemed to favor the repeated syllable. Puka Puka meant Hole Hole in Polynesian dialects. Yet her pastorate was never limited to the chains of the Marshall Islands. After some time she had secured permission to go to the eastern Carolines. Indeed, she had been at Truk when the word came that the Mission Board was sending out a ship, this ship, that was to serve the mission field and, strangely enough, to become her floating parsonage. She had gone by Navy plane to Ponape and from there by ship to Truk and eventually to Kusaie, as opportunity offered. After the first shock, the Navy men were rather taken with the idea of having a lady aboard their ship. The word had been passed to quit swearing and manfully they had adhered to it. An officer had hastily vacated his quarters so she might have his cabin. When a short circuit had caused a small fire and she, clad in a Japanese kimono, had come dashing out for help, the crew had really been nonplussed, for she had shouted first in Marshallese and then in Kusaien, forgetting in her excitement that English was the language of the ship!

She had been ashore at Kusaie when the *Morning Star VI* arrived from the States. An old man, who had been a crewman on *Morning Star IV* back in his youth before the turn of the century, had been keeping watch for days from a mountain ledge. The main islands of Kusaie are high, green volcanic mountains rising from the floor of the ocean. They can be seen from twenty-five miles at sea. All are clustered on a single reef. The Japanese called Kusaie the Pearl of the Pacific. Many visitors, like Eleanor herself, believed these to be the most beautiful islands in the world. But, as in Eden, there was a serpent. Two *Morning Stars,* the II and III, under skilled captains but with adverse winds, had gone on the reef here and been broken to splinters.

It was on a Sunday afternoon that the old man had shouted, "I have seen the *Morning Star!* It is coming! The *Star* is coming!"

A little boy had run all the way up the mountainside to the mission to tell the glad news. Many of the islanders were in the church attending afternoon service. Eleanor and Queen Hattie, the Kasra of Kusaie, had taken their places on the sea wall. They did not quite believe, but they were waiting. It was too soon to expect the *Star* all the way from the Marshalls! Could the old man's vision be relied upon? He had been famous for his eyesight even in this land of keen-eyed seamen, but he was very old now and, even if he had seen a sail, how could he know it was the mission ship, new to these waters?

But the Kusaiens believed! They were coming around the mountain from all directions. The shore was thronged with people. Canoes were being launched. It was too far for them to venture out to the break in the reef where the *Star* must enter. Only one went to meet the ship . . . if ship there were. This was the canoe of the man whose pride it was that he knew the pass better than anyone else—the unofficial pilot of Kusaie. The rest were waiting. They would be here in the inner harbor to welcome the *Star* when it came "home." There were shouts from the people. Eleanor had never seen such enthusiasm. Something of the ancient spirit of the islanders was let loose in this hour of jubilation.

Now others had seen the speck on the horizon, first her sails, long before anyone could make out her hull. Then someone saw the pennant at her masthead. They could not tell its color at this distance, but they knew its shape—the blue pennant with the white dove that had flown at the masthead of every *Morning Star*. With the pilot in the lead, she was coming through the pass now, cautiously, with shortened sails, as became a sailing ship in this land of reefs. Once through the pass, she put on more canvas and bore down on them like a conquering hero. The people went wild. Every canoe was in the water. Eleanor, in the Queen's canoe, clung to the outrigger as the Queen's men paddled madly to be first aboard the *Star*. Eleanor was shouting, too, calling her welcome to their own ship! Cambridge was another world. She was part and parcel of this world, of this company, one with them in their hour of great joy.

"She comes! She comes!" The words were a chant, repeated over and over in the rich cadence of the island voices. Then she was close in and the canoes were all about her. Eleanor felt herself lifted from the canoe to the deck. Queen Hattie leaped lightly aboard, scorning help. Islanders never miss their step in a swaying boat. It is almost an inherited agility, something no landsman, no city dweller, is likely to learn.

There were handclasps between welcomers and welcomees. Captain Price Lewis and his youthful crew were bearded like pirates. They had had a rough passage out from Honolulu and a bad storm before reaching Kwajalein. The sails were worn and patched. It was well that rigging was woven wire. Rope must have parted under the strain. They were bone weary and thankful to be here. The young captain watched with satisfaction as the anchors were dropped over the side.

"What do you want more than anything else?" Eleanor asked the captain and crewmen as they were paddled to the mission station by the shore.

"A drink of water, a bath and a shave, and something to eat besides canned beans!" the captain answered laughing.

"You can have all of these!" she told them. What luck that there was something special for them! Only yesterday her cook had fried a great batch of doughnuts, and they were safely stored in tin boxes to protect them against the ever-present cockroaches.

Being Sunday there could be no noisy celebration; shouts of welcome did not count! But there was rejoicing everywhere on the four inhabited islands of the Kusaie group and the word was going out, almost by frigate bird, it seemed, over thousands of miles of sea. Soon on every island in the Carolines they would be saying, "The *Star* is back! The *Star* is back!"

There had been no *Morning Star* in forty-two years, but what is forty-two years to island memories? Their fathers and grandfathers had known the *Stars*. Many had sailed on these mission ships. If one was wrecked, another came. There had always been a *Star*—they were sure there always would be. On one atoll the people smiled proudly at one another. Their thatched, temporary chapel was ready. It had been swept and cared for daily. They *knew* their missionaries would return. They were prepared.

Faith in the islands was not as a grain of mustard seed, but as the coconuts, which, once brought to these islands from some distant homeland, floated from atoll to atoll and planted themselves in seemingly inhospitable soil, to grow into great trees to nourish the people.

CHAPTER III

The Tradition of the *Star*

THAT HAD BEEN in February of 1948, when the *Star* had come to Kusaie. Eleanor had long since ceased to think of such a thing as winter, for it was always summer here so close to the equator. Seasons were marked, not on the calendar, but by the ripening of the breadfruit and the coming of the trade winds. Many episodes of her long years of service in the islands had been forgotten, but not the arrival of *Morning Star VI!* She retained a vivid picture of the bronzed young men sitting about the table at the old mission at Lelu in Kusaie, devouring the delicious doughnuts fried in coconut oil, feasting on fresh papaya, and being polite about breadfruit.

She had wanted to hear all about that voyage, from Boston to the Panama Canal, where they had picked up a mascot, Henrietta, the ship's cat; thence to the Galápagos Islands, famed for their turtles in the old whaling days; then on to Honolulu; and the last and most dangerous leg of the journey, nearly three thousand miles from Honolulu southwest to Kwajalein and to Kusaie.

All the young crewmen had had some sailing experience, either in the Navy or in pleasure boats, but it had been quite another thing, they found, sailing a sixty-three-foot schooner across the Pacific.

Captain Price Lewis smiled reminiscently. "It was no picnic, Miss Wilson, with only five of us to sail her, but I wouldn't have missed it for anything in the world. It . . . it

sort of made you feel as if you were part of something, perhaps of the old tradition of the sea."

Daniel Akaka, the engineer, nodded. He understood better than the others, for he was pure Polynesian and came
of people who had a longer maritime tradition than these
young Americans.

"I tell you, ma'am," young Captain Lewis went on, "I
came to really admire those old Yankee sea captains who
came out here around 1790, wasn't it? They were explorers
as much as merchantmen! With their charts, mostly blank
in this area, and their old instruments, they went it blind.
Lord—excuse me, ma'am—they couldn't find their longitude
within a hundred miles. And when they went ashore for
food and water, like as not they would run into cannibals!"

Eleanor had laughed outright at their enthusiasm for their
seafaring predecessors. She knew something of this feeling.
Whatever hardships a modern missionary encountered, they
were as nothing compared with those of the firstcomers.

"And what about our missionaries?" she asked with a
twinkle. "A sea captain had at least his own ship in which
to get away and some twenty able crewmen and muskets!
When Dr. Snow and his party came to this island, their
chartered ship just set them ashore and sailed away. The
missionaries had no knowledge of when or how they could
ever leave, and their only protection was a letter from King
Kamehameha III of Hawaii recommending them to the native kings!"

The men whistled. Young Loren, son of Admiral Miller,
spoke up. He was radioman aboard the *Star*. "I guess they
must have counted on the good Lord to look after them," he
said seriously. "Only people who were sure of that could
have faced such risks and such hardships with so much courage. When was that, Miss Wilson?"

"Well, they left Boston in 1851. But unlike you, they had
to go around the Horn. It took them four months to reach
Honolulu. They went through hardships on that voyage
quite like those of the crew of the *Bounty*. It was 1852 when

they came to Kusaie. They didn't have their own ship until 1857. Do you know who brought the first *Star* out here?"

They shook their heads.

"Young Dr. Hiram Bingham, Jr., son of our first missionary to Hawaii! He was born in Hawaii and spoke any number of island dialects. He brought Hawaiian Christian teachers with him. Without them, I have often wondered if the mission could have taken such root."

"I see," Captain Lewis said. "The Kusaiens and the other islanders felt a kinship with them. I guess they had small reason to trust white men, from some of the tales I've read of how the whalers behaved out here."

Eleanor flushed. The whalers, too, had been New Englanders.

"Yes, our missionaries had their troubles because of such things. Some whaling captain had stolen a chief's wife shortly before they came, and it had led to a very bloody war. It took some time to convince the islanders that our missionaries were not the same kind of people."

The young crewmen looked out the mission window at the blackness of the tropic night. Two of them were brothers, Joe and Al Linish, bent on adventure. They could not see the jungle, but they could feel it through the very pores of their skin. And there was a fragrance, at once alluring and terrifying. Every sense told them they were in an unfamiliar world.

"There is a timelessness about these islands," Captain Lewis said thoughtfully. "At home, you are so aware of the present active moment that the past is pretty hazy. But out here. . . ."

The other young men nodded.

"Time has small significance to a native islander," Eleanor explained. "That's the first thing we Americans must learn. To them the past, present, and future all flow together in one stream. That is why tradition is so important to them. That was why the coming of *Morning Star VI* was the cause of so much rejoicing."

"Now I understand!" Lewis exclaimed. "It makes their history and their dreams real. It . . . it's as if the first *Morning Star* had come again."

A strange bird screamed from out of the thick growth of trees. The wind made the pandanus leaves rustle like stiff silk. The air was heavy with the fragrance of the plumieras. In the distance they heard singing, a three-part song, and this time not a hymn, but some old island melody antedating the coming of the missionaries. The brothers looked at their fellow crewmen. Each understood what the others felt. It was to experience these things that they had enlisted for small wages to bring the *Morning Star VI* out to Kusaie.

"What was she like, the first *Star?*" young Miller asked.

"She was a brigantine," Eleanor said.

"That means she was a square-rigger except that her mains'le was rigged fore and aft," Captain Lewis said. "That was a very popular rig with the old whalers. Guess it was suited to long ocean voyages. How big was she?"

"About one hundred and fifty tons, I believe. I know she was a two-master, Massachusetts built, and a real beauty, the old accounts say. She was a thing of wonder to many of the people here, the first ship some had ever seen. Even the whalers had touched at relatively few of the countless atolls."

"What happened to her?" Captain Lewis asked with interest.

"After ten years of service in the islands, she was sold to carry freight to China. No word of her was ever received after she left Honolulu."

A silence fell over the young mariners. They had had a close enough call in the storm between Hawaii and Kwajalein. The thought of another *Star* lost in a storm struck home.

"And *Morning Star II?*" the captain asked quickly. It was not good for the morale of his crew to think too much of disasters when they still had to sail a small schooner over many miles of empty sea.

Eleanor hesitated. "She was wrecked right here on the reef

at Kusaie," she said regretfully. "She lasted only three years. You see, that was before the days of steam. She had almost reached safety when adverse winds blew her on the reef."

Lewis nodded understandingly. "You can't claw off a lee shore with a square-rigger like you can with a schooner. That's why the schooner replaced the square-rigger in the Atlantic coastwise trade. I guess the square sails were better for the long haul of a Pacific voyage."

They looked at her expectantly. As crew of the *Star VI* her story was of the keenest interest to them. Eleanor hesitated. Sailing the mission ships had been one long succession of hardships, and they were so young that they might not share her feeling that her life was in the Lord's hands and when one went about His business, it did not matter under what circumstances. One carried the work forward as long as he could, then other willing hands took it up.

"*Morning Star III* went ashore at the same place some years later," she said. "But within the year—that was 1884— a new and finer *Star* was built. The fourth *Star* is still remembered by the old people in the islands. She was a barkentine, a three-master, with one set of square sails and the rest schooner-rigged. She had auxiliary steam power and an iron smokestack as tall as her masts. The old man who first sighted your sail this morning once served aboard her. She was the famous *Star* with the figurehead of a woman with an open Bible in her hands."

"I know!" Price Lewis said. "I saw a picture of her in your American Board office in Boston when I signed on for this cruise. She had on a white dress and high button shoes!"

Eleanor nodded. "That was high style in 1884. They were even common when I was a child. They went with the surrey with the fringe on top."

The young men looked politely astonished. How could they think back to high button shoes and the horse and buggy when they had grown up in the air age?

"I bet that smokestack really astonished the islanders," the Hawaiian engineer said.

"Not only the islanders," Eleanor had assured them. "Her smokestack looked so much like a mast that when they passed another ship in the Straits of Magellan, with all sail furled, someone bellowed at them through a megaphone demanding what power they had!"

"The Straits of Magellan!" Loren exclaimed. "Wow!"

"It was either that or go around Old Cape Stiff," Price Lewis said laughing. "Not many vessels cared to try the Straits until they had steam. Too many ships were lost there. Did you think she came through the Panama Canal the way we did?"

There had been a roar of laughter. No one was so bold as to ask what date the canal was opened. It was in 1914, but none of them knew for sure. Somewhere around the First World War, wasn't it? To most of them that was as remote as Dewey at Manila and Teddy Roosevelt at San Juan Hill.

"Did she come to grief, too?" Al Linish asked.

"No, the reef was conquered at last by steam," Eleanor told them. "The *Star* used her sails on the ocean journeys and saved her fuel for cruising close to the islands. She had a long and honorable history. She was sold in 1900 as past use."

Eleanor's thoughts winged back to the other *Star* that she herself had known.

"I saw the next *Star* leave Boston in 1904," she said. "I was one of the owners. I was just turned thirteen, and I felt like a real shipping magnate."

The boys laughed. They had all seen the little yellowed certificates, shares in the *Morning Stars,* sold for ten cents apiece to the children in Congregational Sunday Schools.

"She sailed out of Boston under the Christian flag and with the blue mission pennant with its white dove at her masthead. She still had to go around the Horn. And she was welcomed here in Kusaie just as you were today!"

There was quiet in the room. What a strong web of tradition was woven about all the *Morning Stars!* They felt it keenly, this crew that had just brought out the *Star VI* in the wake of her predecessors.

Price Lewis spoke for all of them. "And now we have *Star VI*, two-masted schooner, sixty-three and a half foot overall, twenty-nine tons burden, with a three-cylinder diesel motor, built at Boothbay as the yacht *Norseman,* of Boston, sailed from Boston for the Pacific, July 27, 1947. May the good Lord keep her safe, and especially off the reef here at Kusaie!"

The young crewmen could hardly keep their eyes open. For the past five days they had scarcely been off watch, snatching cat naps and eating cold food as they could. One by one they said good night and went back to their quarters aboard the *Star.* Miss Wilson regretted that the war had destroyed their larger mission house at Lelu, the port village of Kusaie. She had no suitable place to lodge them ashore. The singing had stopped now, but the fragrance of the jungle night still reached them as they rowed the dinghy in silence to the *Star.*

When they had gone, the mission was very still. Myriad insects beat against the screens as if demanding entrance. Eleanor thought of the Japanese legend of Princess Firefly's lovers, who came nightly to seek fire in the hot flame of the candle. But mostly she thought with deep gratitude of the safe arrival of the *Star,* with her fine, able young captain and crew. They were so strong and confident. It was heartening in view of the work of rebuilding the missions that lay ahead. Once again the mission stations of Micronesia, like jewels on a chain, would be linked together from Truk to Ebon, from the central Carolines to the easternmost Marshalls.

What a wonderful thing tradition was, she thought, as tough and enduring as the jungle lianas that would bear a man's whole weight and never fail him in his climb. A *Star* would never fail to sail these seas in pursuit of her high purpose—to bring the word of God to the devoted people of the high islands and the low atolls. She was a part of this tradition. It was something to make one both humble and proud. It gave to a missionary's life meaning and purpose. The tradition must not fail, for it had deep roots in the life of these islands. It was a part of the people's faith.

She had gone to sleep that night in Kusaie utterly content.

CHAPTER IV

One Step at a Time

THE SUN HAD SET over Kwajalein and still Eleanor sat by the ship's rail. What memories had crowded into her consciousness like pictures thrown on a screen! The crewmen had now eaten their scant supper and were squatting on the forward deck, realizing with characteristic island sensitivity that their lady missionary wished to be alone. They had not yet been able to grasp that she was captain of the ship. Sailing a ship was man's work, a thing for which women were utterly unfit. Traditionally the steering of the ship, the navigation, was the special prerogative of a chosen few whose knowledge was jealously guarded and passed down from blood kin to blood kin, in the island manner of succession. Even today when, under the teaching of the missionaries and the civil authorities, many island customs had become obsolete, still the men who understood wave patterns and could steer by them and the stars were men apart—men who were admired by all the Marshallese for this ancient skill.

Anliri, the island sailing master of the *Star,* looked moodily at Freddy Milne, the fair-skinned boatswain. A redheaded Scots trader two generations back had left Freddy a quarter of his blood and with it something of a Scot's stubbornness, his stocky build and a skin too fair for a true Marshallese. There was no need to speak their thoughts. They knew what would happen with Mother Wilson aboard! Everything at the mission was always spotlessly clean. She would demand the same cleanliness aboard this ship.

Lau, a crewman, spoke in Marshallese softly, for fear his words might reach the lady back aft. "Bukmeto left the galley very dirty. Dr. Hanlin maybe didn't see, but Mother Wilson will! Very early tomorrow I will start to scrub!"

"Good," Freddy, the boatswain, responded. But his tone was half-hearted. He knew it was his task to keep the *Star* bright and shining, and he knew he had not done it. Dr. Hanlin had been too busy and preoccupied with his work to check on it, and it had been so easy to grow careless.

"How will we go to sea again?" Clement, the island engineer, asked. "I can't make the engine work. Japanese motors were all different." He shook his head in utter despair.

They all turned to look at Luckabudge. He was a very simple man with no pretensions to any special talents, except in reading the clouds, at which he was always consulted by the sailing master. But he had one particular gift which all recognized. He was a devout Christian and had an infallible sense of right and wrong. Slow to make up his mind and still slower to speak, when he did voice an opinion the other crewmen had a way of listening.

"We will sail," Luckabudge said confidently. "The Lord wants a ship to bring Bibles to the islands. Always He has sent us a ship. If there is no man to be her captain, then the Lord will teach Mother Wilson how to read the stars. It is not a secret any more, for it is written in books. Dr. Hanlin read the books, and he even taught Freddy how to measure how high the sun climbs at noon. It cannot be too hard, or I do not think Freddy could do it!" Soft laughter rippled over the forepeak. Freddy was, indeed, no scholar. Luckabudge could read the Bible quite as well as he.

"It is not necessary to be wise to serve the Lord," Luckabudge continued. "Many of the disciples were fishermen like us. The wisdom they needed was given to them a little at a time. It will be so with us."

They all looked at Luckabudge with new respect. It was surprising how he made things plain to them, in phrases they could well understand. Still, a woman to captain a ship! It went against the grain of the Marshallese male. True, inheritance was through the female line. A child belonged to his mother's clan, not to that of his father. The right to the land and the fruits of the land was inherited purely through the mother's line. There was no question as to a child's maternal rights. But many things remained a male prerogative, and the management of a ship was one of these. In all their long tradition of priest-astronomers there had never been a woman to whom the secrets of the craft had been entrusted. But that, Anliri, the island captain, reflected, was before the coming of books. With books there were no secrets once a man had learned to read English. There were few books in Marshallese. It was embarrassing to many island adults that their children, now at the government or mission schools, could already read English better than they.

Boaz, another crewman, grunted his disapproval of all innovation. He did not hold with women having anything to do with boats. They had enough to do at home. Boaz had so many children back on the island of Likiep that he had lost count of them. Indeed, when they were in port, every man of the crew had some private worry. Anliri had a sick wife over on Carlos Island. Freddy's wife needed him back on Ebon Island. Bukmeto, the cook, was back in Majuro getting his first set of store teeth. Clement worried about his engine. No one knew much about Lau, who kept rather to himself. Luckabudge was the balance wheel. He seemed motivated by some guiding power that did not move the others. He was happy working on the *Star* no matter what duty was assigned him, from scrubbing the deck to cleaning out the bilge. Only Dr. Hanlin had understood. To all the crewmen, working on the *Star* was more than a means of livelihood. It was a chance to serve the Lord. But Luckabudge brought to it a special devotion. It gave to the gaunt islander a dignity that others were quick to recognize, if not always to emulate.

Without a word being said or any agreement reached, it was understood that on the morrow work would begin to

set the *Star* in order, to make all shipshape aboard the mission schooner. They hoped to do this before the lady missionary should notice how much it was needed. There was
the matter of a man's pride.

So the talk went among the crew as the lady skipper sat
alone wrestling with her problem. Eleanor Wilson reasoned
it out a step at a time. There must be a ship to visit the
island missions or they would be cut off from one another
and the church's help. They had a ship. It must be put in
shape to sail, and someone must sail it. If there was no one
else to do it, then she must do it. It was her inescapable duty.
The sacredness of duty had been the cornerstone of her early
teaching. It was more honorable to try and fail than not
to try at all.

But to take in one's charge the lives of others! That was
the part that terrified her. Suppose, once out of sight of land,
they were lost. Would she not be responsible? It was all well
enough to say one could trust the native crew. For seamanship, yes, but for distance navigation, no! Not long ago a
Marshallese sailing craft bound on a journey between two
of the Marshall Islands had shown up at Kusaie in the Carolines four hundred miles off course. Another, given up for
lost, had landed in the New Hebrides! The old skills of sailing by wave patterns were vanishing. She knew she could
not rely wholly on these.

She thought of the *Morning Stars* that had piled up on
reefs even when under the command of able captains. Then
it came to her with a sense almost of shock that not a life
had been lost while any *Star* flew the mission flag. The first
Star was lost in the China Sea, but it had been sold by the
Board before that voyage. The fourth *Star,* and the fifth,
escaped disaster, and this schooner had already come safely
through many dangers. It was necessary to have faith. She
thought of Saint Paul in the shipwreck, when he prayed to
the Lord and laid hold on a raft. He had come safely ashore.

One did not always have to succeed, Eleanor reasoned, but
certainly a servant of God must at least try to do the task

assigned. The only alternative she had was to tell the Mission
Board and the people of the islands that she could not do
this thing. She could see the look of hurt and bewilderment
in the eyes of her parishioners. She had never failed them,
had never flinched at facing any problem they brought to
her in all the years she had lived among them. She could
not fail them now.

She would take it a step at a time. First, the ship must
be made spick-and-span. Even in her first cursory glance she
had noted how dirty it was. The crewmen were far from im-
maculate. The Marshallese people at home are spotlessly
clean. They bathe daily, and the women keep their cotton
clothing starched and ironed. But men, away from their
women, grow careless. It is the same the world over. She
shuddered to think of cockroaches in the ship's galley and
even more unwelcome visitors in their sleeping quarters.

At least, the housekeeping fell within her experience.
Then there would be the matter of discipline. As a missionary, her authority was unquestioned. Would it be the same
aboard ship? They would be polite, but would they obey
her? She would have to be careful not to offend their masculine pride. Her hand touched the coil of wire that served
as the ship's rail and came away soiled. She looked at the
deck. It had not been washed down that day and the canvas
lashed to the boom overhead looked mildewed.

Tomorrow she would inspect the ship fore and aft, topside
and below decks, and they would all set to work. Once the
men were busy, she would go ashore and see what she could
do about the ship's equipment. She was used enough to
having to work with mended machinery. Everything de-
teriorated in the tropics. Salt corroded almost anything made
of metal. Clocks had a way of getting out of gear. One
learned to tell time largely by the sun. Cockroaches ate the
books and cloth, not to mention the food. Nothing remained
long in good condition.

Then her mind turned to the knottiest problem, that of
learning to navigate a ship. Dr. Hanlin had learned by him-

self from books. She had the textbook that the young coast guardsman back at Majuro had insisted on giving her. After all, men who knew little enough of this science had crossed the ocean. Hadn't she heard that Columbus was not a navigator, only a coastwise pilot? And what of young Captain Jones who brought the *Mayflower* over the stormy North Atlantic passage in the dead of winter? Stories she had heard came back to her; of refugees from Latvia sailing leaking boats thousands of miles to freedom; of young Americans escaping from Red China in a top-heavy junk they had stolen from a Chinese war lord. And they had crossed the entire Pacific! Perhaps, as the Chinese believed, the great eye painted on either side of the junk's prow had seen the way! She could almost wish that there was an eye on the *Morning Star* to watch out for coral reefs.

She became aware now of the world around her. Lost in her thoughts, she had forgotten about everything else. The sun had gone down behind great banks of cumulus clouds. The colors of the clouds—salmon, rose, and gray—were reflected in the now placid waters of the lagoon. There were just enough ripples to make a beautiful changing play of color. The white schooner and, had she known it, she herself in her white dress and with her soft white hair, were bathed in the warm colors of the red end of the spectrum.

She turned to look at the softer colors in the east. There great white clouds scudded like full-rigged ships before the wind, each caught in the reflection of the western sky. How startling was their likeness to the ships of a century ago—to the *Morning Stars* that had sailed these seas. And there were five of them, one following the other.

"Oh!" she exclaimed and rose to take another look. Then for the first time she noticed the crew on the forward deck.

"Anliri! Luckabudge! What do those clouds look like to you?" She went forward to speak with them. The six island men scanned the sky. Then Anliri turned to her.

"Like ships, Mother Wilson, old-time ships," he said, pleased that she had consulted him.

"Like *Morning Stars* long ago," Luckabudge said reverently. "See, Mother Wilson, one, two, three, four, five; and now comes our *Star!* Look, far off on the horizon!"

Eleanor gasped. Was it a mirage? An image of their ship reflected on the clouds? Such things were known to happen. Islands appeared as if lifted out of the sea. The clouds were mirrors. Surely she did not imagine that the sixth cloud-ship was their own schooner, slight of hull, two-masted, with fore and aft rig! She was following the others in a long line, and they were all sailing toward them out of the northeast, on the course from Honolulu by which all mission ships had come. The faces of the crewmen were beaming.

"Luckabudge is right," Freddy said solemnly. "He said we would sail again."

Eleanor's hand gripped the *Star's* guardrail. Her inheritance was more from the Puritan than from the Gael. She did not believe in signs and omens, but it was strangely comforting to see the *Star VI* there in the clouds sailing proudly on its course. They exchanged glances, the island crew and their missionary. There was something new in Mother Wilson's manner, something that had not been there before. It was a thing without substance, but it *was* there. Anliri knew! She was the Captain of the ship.

"Mother Wilson," he said, "tomorrow we will make your ship shine. We are sorry. When no one noticed, we did not do our work. We will scrub. We will paint. We will make all clean. You will not be ashamed. Maybe United States Navy can fix our engine. They can fix very big engines. Maybe also little engines."

Clement tried to look more hopeful than he felt. Eleanor followed suit.

"Tomorrow I will start to study navigation," she said. "I am sure some of the Navy officers can teach me. After all, Dr. Hanlin taught himself. And Freddy, you know how to shoot the sun at noontime. Dr. Hanlin told me so."

Freddy flushed. "Only sometimes a little, Mother Wilson. Sometimes the numbers do not come out right. One time,

Dr. Hanlin tells me I am not in these islands. I am in Japan! I make a big mistake. But I try!" he added brightly.

"Mother Wilson," Luckabudge said solicitously, "you have had no supper. Lau, warm up some beans and corned beef for Mother Wilson."

At first Eleanor shook her head. At this moment she felt she could not face the canned food, half warmed in Lau's not too clean skillet. She appreciated their concern. She longed for a cool drink from a green coconut, but there were none on board. She felt a sudden faintness. She must eat something, and she might as well get used to ship's fare.

"Bring me what you have,' she said.

Luckabudge himself ran to fetch the food. Lau was already in the galley. She ate her beans and some rather crumbly ship's biscuit and nibbled at the corned beef.

"It is all we have," Lau said regretfully. "Dr. Hanlin had not time to buy food for the ship. We eat mostly fish and rice like in Japanese times."

Eleanor found she was hungry and that the unappetizing food tasted well enough. Suddenly she remembered that she had had little breakfast and no lunch at all. She ate with what she feared was unladylike haste.

When Lau took the plate, she stood up again and walked once around the deck. Off to the north, there was a rift in the clouds and a star shone through.

"Freddy," she said, "isn't that the North Star? It's at just the right height, eight degrees. You know the North Star is as high above the horizon, I've heard, as the watcher is above the equator."

The crew listened respectfully. Freddy nodded, whether he knew or not. After all, he had only taken sun shots and had left the stars to Dr. Hanlin.

"See," Luckabudge whispered, "even without a book, a lady can tell the stars just like a man."

Eleanor smiled. Perhaps navigation was not a matter meant exclusively for the male sex. She knew a few stars and, with a good star map, she could learn the rest. She would have to, if she were to captain this ship!

She was cramped from long sitting. She took a turn or two in the narrow space around the cockpit. An odd sense of possession came over her. Was there some magic that made a commander part and parcel of his ship? Her back was very straight now. Fear had left her. They were safe at anchor. That was enough for tonight. Tomorrow was another day and whatever problems it brought, she would solve them as best she could. First, a taut ship, as the Navy boys said, then to Navy Headquarters for skilled help with her gear. From this moment she must feel confidence in herself, if she was to inspire it in her crew.

"Good night," she called to the men and went below. The air in the master's cabin was stifling. The mattress smelled musty and stale. But the skylight was open and that was all that could be done. Resolutely, Eleanor Wilson lay down on one of the bunks and fell asleep. She did not know that Luckabudge left the airier deck to sleep outside her door. In case she called, like the child Samuel, he could answer, "Here am I!"

CHAPTER V

Sea of Troubles

ELEANOR WOKE BEFORE SUNRISE and looked out. She caught her breath. There serene in the east shone Venus, the Morning Star, watching over her namesake on the lagoon below. What a good omen! She lay back and closed her eyes. She fell into a deep sleep. When she woke again, she was startled. What were those strange sounds over her head? Was it rain on the thatched roof of her mission school? Was it the wind whipping the fronds of the pandanus tree against her one-room house at Rong Rong? Were the coconut palms snapping in a gale? This was the month of March, the season for high winds.

She sat bolt upright and struck her head sharply on the upper bunk. She stifled a cry. Where was she? In twenty years of missionary work she had slept in strange and uncanny places—in a church set in a graveyard and, perhaps worse, in a house where human beings lived beneath the floor. But where was she now?

Then she heard the droning of planes and the sound of the motor of an LST. She heard the exchange of hails between the Navy boys and her own crew. She felt the schooner rock in the backwash of the passing ship. She was aboard the *Morning Star!* The sounds over her head were not made by rain or wind but by bare feet running on the deck! The realization came as something of a shock. In the excitement and fatigue of yesterday, she had not thought what it would be like to wake morning after morning without solid earth beneath her, not even a strip of coral a few feet above the water.

The musty smell of the mattress on which she had slept offended her. Indeed, there were many strange odors which reached her. She was well accustomed to strange smells, but the odor of unaired bedding was intolerable to her. No amount of living in the orient under makeshift conditions could take away from a New England lady her love of cleanliness and order. This mattress would be on deck in the sun within the hour!

She heard voices now. She recognized that of Anliri, the sailing master, calling to the men in Marshallese to hurry. Now she knew why there was so much coming and going on deck overhead. Plumbing in these islands had a way of getting out of order. Aboard the *Star* it had all but ceased to exist. There was a hand bowl in the captain's cabin opposite hers that would drain, but the "head" had long since ceased to function. This was a small inconvenience when only men were aboard. The islanders by long-established custom used the sea. It was only in deference to mission standards that they had built a "head" (something of a misnomer, as it was located on the fantail)—a wobbly structure of two-by-fours, which might serve in a calm but which would be hazardous in a squall. A strip of canvas gave privacy of a sort. Eleanor shuddered at the thought of using it. She recalled reading the words of the great architect, Frank Lloyd Wright, who said not to laugh at the water closet; that it had given dignity to life. How right he was!

There was a timid knock at the door and Luckabudge said, "Mother Wilson, here is water for you to wash, nice fresh water from shore." Obviously this was a luxury aboard the *Star,* as it had been on sailing ships since time began.

Eleanor smoothed her dress—a sad mass of wrinkles for she had slept in it—and ran a comb through her disordered hair. Then she opened the door and said in what she hoped was a cheerful, early morning sort of voice, "Thank you, Luckabudge. I will be on deck directly."

She washed in the bucket. The fresh water was infinitely refreshing. Then she fixed her hair. It was no new thing to sleep in the clothes which she had worn all day, offensive as this was to her. Indeed, among the islanders it was the common custom. Few of them owned sleeping garments, and here aboard ship plainly it would be a necessity, as she could not know when an emergency might arise. She smiled, remembering the two Miss Baldwins of the mission school on Kusaie before the war who always slept fully dressed in case they should be called in the night. Perish the thought that a Victorian lady should ever appear in a "wrapper"! The clothing she wore was not much of a burden, however. She had learned quickly that to live on the equator, it must be reduced to a minimum. Luckily the mission girls at Majuro had kept her rather meager wardrobe of faded print cotton dresses in excellent order, but their strenuous laundry methods were hard on fabrics, for in the age-old way they pounded them with paddles. After the pounding came the added hazard of scorching from their old-fashioned Japanese charcoal irons!

She took special pains this morning to make herself spruce and neat. What was there about a ship that demanded that all be in order? "Shipshape and Bristol fashion" was the expression, wasn't it? She stood a moment, listening. The sound of running feet had ceased. That meant that the crew was at breakfast, up forward she hoped. Resolutely she climbed the stairs. Must she learn to call it a ladder? The rear deck, no, the aft deck it should be called, was deserted. Courtesy and natural modesty were a part of the Marshallese character. Now the eyes of all the crew were averted. Setting her teeth, she walked over the jerry-rigged platform out on to the fantail. This was her first lesson in navigation at sea. But what would one do in a storm?

She looked about the deck for a likely place to eat breakfast. Just then Lau came out of the galley, beaming. He had a dish of fish and rice in his hand.

"You sit in the cockpit, Mother Wilson. It is very fine for you there. Here is your breakfast."

"Thank you, Lau." She tried not to look disappointed. Cereal and canned milk were available now from Navy stores, and she had come to think of breakfast in American terms. Well, she had eaten fish and rice for seven years in Japan, if, indeed, they were always lucky enough to have fish to flavor their rice. Under Japanese rule the islanders had grown accustomed to this diet and suffered now if they could not get rice in exchange for their copra. Rice would not grow on low coral atolls. How Eleanor longed for a glass of fresh sweet milk. But even here in Kwajalein it was not available. West of Honolulu milk came in cans or was "reconstituted" from powdered milk. There was no grazing for cattle and the expense of importing hay was prohibitive.

She ate hastily and passed the plate and the tin spoon back to Lau. He might this morning have given her chopsticks and she would scarcely have noticed. Her mind was on the business of the day. Yet she must not be too brusque. It was this quality in Americans that startled and offended the island peoples. She must move softly, taking things casually a step at a time, so that they sensed beforehand what she would ask of them.

"Lau," she said, "is it not time for morning prayers?"

The crew came without being called and gathered around the cockpit quietly. All of them were Christians and most of them were members of the island churches. Only Clement and the absent Bukmeto did not, at this itme, hold this coveted honor. Island standards for church membership are much more rigid than in most stateside churches. Something of the militant Puritanism of the first missionaries still remained in the islands. Yet today it was not the Congregational Church nor the American Board of Foreign Missions that made the rules, but the island churches themselves. Members must not smoke, and nonchurch members must not pray in public. Clement could not bring himself to forego the one small luxury of a cigarette. Secretly Eleanor felt it was a harsh rule, but it had a definite economic aspect. Where the money income of the islanders was so small, it was not wise to cultivate a habit whose gratification meant real sacrifice to them and to their families. Copra—dried coconut—was their only crop, and it took all their income to feed and clothe their households decently.

The crewmen gathered around their missionary with bowed heads. Then they dropped to the deck with the grace and ease of a people to whom chairs are alien. Eleanor wondered for a moment what text to choose. Then as her eye caught the isles of the circling reef of the atoll, one came to her. She said it aloud. Several heads nodded. It was one of their favorites.

"Psalm ninety-seven," Eleanor said. " 'The Lord reigneth, let the multitude of the isles be glad thereof.' "

When the amens had been said, she braced herself for her first nonclerical assignment aboard this ship.

"Anliri, you and the men know that we have all been given a task here that at the moment seems beyond our strength. With Dr. Hanlin gone, there is no one but ourselves to sail the *Star* to our mission stations."

Nods greeted this statement. They knew, and they had made up their minds before their lady missionary arrived, that the *Star* would not sail again until the Mission Board sent out a man for captain. Eleanor sensed their attitude and knew it would not be easy to change it. Dr. Hanlin had been, like herself, a member of the clergy. He had not been a seaman, nor did he like the sea. Indeed, life aboard ship had been hard on him. But at least Dr. Hanlin was a man. Mother Wilson was a woman. That was quite another thing in the eyes of the crewmen. They would humor her and protect her, but they had no mind to put to sea under her command in a boat that was badly battered by service, with an engine and radio that were not working, and with sails that had seen their best days, Eleanor felt their dismay at even having her aboard.

She plunged into her speech. What she must say was not

a matter for rhetoric, but was dictated by two simple things: hard circumstance and her unshakable faith that if this _were_ their work, help would be forthcoming. It was this faith that had brought her to these islands for her life's work.

"You are all Christians. You all know your Bibles. You know if the Lord means us to sail the _Star_ and do His work, He will strengthen our hands. We must do all we can ourselves and pray fervently for His help." She paused to let this thought sink into their consciousness.

"When Jesus began his ministry on earth he had only twelve disciples. They were not learned men. Many of them were fishermen, as you are. They set out to carry the gospel to the whole world. It certainly did not seem possible for them to succeed, but they did not despair. Nor did they question their orders. And only one of them failed."

There was no need to elucidate. Island church members loved their Bibles and knew the familiar stories well.

"Our task is much simpler than that of the disciples," Eleanor continued. "We have only to carry on the work here in these islands; at first, only on this atoll. We must be content with that until our ship is fitted for the sea." She hesitated, appealing to their masculine instinct to protect her.

"I am only a woman. I must depend for seamanship on all of you, especially on you, Anliri, for you are the sailing master; and on you, Luckabudge, for you understand the meaning of the clouds. I know you and the men can handle the _Star_ in any weather."

Anliri swelled visibly. He was a little, old man, but the pride of his ancient craft was strong in him. In the days before the missionaries came, the navigator was a man of high rank and of tremendous prestige. Furthermore, his knowledge was a secret, jealously guarded from all but a few selected kinsmen.

"Freddy," she addressed the descendant of the Scottish trader, "you are the bo'sun." She smiled, thankful she knew the correct nautical term. It was hard not to smile at Freddy, even now when she was trying to be grave. His personality differed widely from that of a typical islander. He could think of a thousand complaints that would never have occurred to a pure Marshallese. She, therefore, tried to sound severe.

"You are responsible for keeping the *Star* spotlessly clean. Cleanliness is next to godliness, and God's ship should certainly have both. When I next come aboard, I want to see this deck scrubbed, and the brass work polished. If you need paint, you know it is in the locker. I want all the mattresses and pillows out in the sun this morning. They must be aired every day until they smell sweet again. There are bad odors everywhere. I want the cabins sprayed with DDT before the cockroaches take over the ship!"

She paused. "I glanced into your galley, Lau. I think you have done very well, especially with Bukmeto, the cook, away. You must have scoured your pots often with sand."

She smiled. "If a woman cannot sail a ship, surely she can keep one clean. And about your clothes. . . . When you are at home, your shirts are always spotless. Why are they so . . ." she hesitated, not wishing to say dirty.

Anliri looked at Clement, Clement looked at Boaz, and Lau looked for help to Luckabudge. Then they all looked down at the deck. Anliri spoke for them all.

"At home our women keep our clothes clean. When we are away, we do not know well how to wash and iron them. But we can take things ashore. Everybody has some cousin on Kwajalein. They will do the laundry for us. We will have everything clean before you come back, Mother Wilson!"

"Good," she said. "Let us say that one week from today we must have the cabins spotless, the engine room cleaned out, and no foul smells aboard the ship. Anliri, I leave this to you and to Freddy. The rest will obey orders and do a good job, I know." She knew the subject must be dropped here.

"I am needed worse on shore than I am here," she said seriously. "I wish, indeed, that I might stay and help you scrub this ship. But I must see if the parts have come to repair our engine; if our clock, I mean our chronometer, is ready; and if our new sails have arrived. And we must stock up the larder. Lau, you can tell me what you need."

Lau looked doleful. "Mother Wilson, we need everything but rice. Dr. Hanlin was very busy. He could not get to the commissary. We have no cereal, no canned milk, almost no sugar, and no canned meat. Only some hard biscuits, and every day we catch some fish. I did not want to trouble Dr. Hanlin," Lau said apologetically.

"I'm sorry, Lau. Two of you men can come ashore with me and bring back what is needed. I hope within a week, I can take care of all our business ashore and have the *Star* ready for at least a short trip."

But somehow her words did not carry quite the ring of conviction she intended. Well, it might take a little longer to get everything ready for their shakedown cruise to some nearby island up the lagoon. The main thing was the engine, of course.

When she had gone below for her small bag, Anliri looked ruefully at his crew. He was too polite to say what he thought. Freddy, who came of a race noted for blunt speech and lack of diplomacy, spoke out.

"It is all for nothing," he said disgustedly. "Why should we polish up the *Star* when she will never go to sea without a new engine, without new sails?" Clement nodded in gloomy agreement.

Lau went to his galley without a word and began to heat water. With his usual humility Luckabudge asked Freddy where he wished him to begin work. Freddy's scornful gesture took in the whole ship. Freddy was an incipient labor agitator. He wanted the conditions of work well understood before he actually rolled up his sleeves. This was an idea quite foreign to island psychology. Islanders, before the European came, had never made any clear distinction between work and play. Housebuilding and canoe making were group activities, joyous occasions for a whole island to share. Therefore, Freddy's ideas were more than a little shocking.

They might well neglect work, for what was the hurry? End-less days stretched ahead of them, and time clocks were unknown. But to question the wishes of chief or missionary or to refuse to do the needed task was un-Marshallese, to say the least. It was a matter of some scandal on Ebon, Freddy's home island, that the people had defied the King, or Iroij, of the island and had gotten away with it. By estab-lished island custom dating back for generations, the Iroij had received a small percentage—a kind of Blue Cross deduc-tion—from the only money crop of the islanders, the sale of their copra. This he dutifully saved and from it paid the hospital expenses of any of his subjects who were sent to the dispensary.

In this feudal practice, the Ebon islanders sensed auto-cratic privilege. Moreover, they thought the amount de-ducted too large! Under American rule, they voted to abol-ish the tax, and from thenceforward each man saved his own money and paid his own hospital expenses. Eleanor had secretly been much amused. Some stubborn Yankee instinct told her that Freddy and his people were right, though ex-perience told her that there was much to be said for the Iroij assuming this responsibility. The sad truth was that most people, islanders or stateside dwellers, were incapable of saving for an emergency. Certainly the carefree Mar-shallese took small thought for the morrow. Still, in this age when modern governments grew rapidly more paternalistic, it was a healthy sign to see individualism growing among her parishioners.

"Who wants to row me ashore?" Eleanor asked pleasantly. The whole crew volunteered as one man. Indeed, the en-thusiastic response might had led one to think they were not anxious to start cleaning up the *Star*.

"Three is quite enough," she said. "Luckabudge, you and Lau may go with me to the commissary, and Boaz may come along to row the dinghy back. I know the rest of you want to start the morning's work."

Chagrin showed on three faces: on Freddy's, on Clement's,

and even on Anliri's. The dinghy was attached by a painter astern. Now it was hauled alongside. The water was calm and it was no trick at all to step down gracefully into the small boat. It was only a five minutes' row to shore. Lucka-budge and Lau shipped their oars and, jumping over the side into the shallow water, ran the dinghy's prow onto the sand. Luckabudge handed Eleanor, dry shod, to the shore.

"When you need us to come for you, how will you call, Mother Wilson?" Luckabudge asked solicitously.

Eleanor laughed. "I'll have to whistle," she said.

Both Lau and Luckabudge looked shocked. Some sense of decorum told them that ladies should not whistle, espe-cially lady missionaries who were ordained ministers and could preach sermons and marry people, and say the service over the dead. Still, how else could a lady call for a boat?

"First we will go to the commissary for supplies," Eleanor said, ignoring the consternation on her crewmen's faces. "Then I must report to the Commanding Officer and the Port Captain. That's the rule. Everyone in charge of a ship must do that, Dr. Hanlin's letter said." They nodded.

"Then I must see about our equipment." She squared her shoulders. A sense of doom settled over her, as if she knew already that all effort would be useless—that there were to be no parts for the engine, no new canvas sails, and no accu-rate timepiece. Her bag felt heavy in spite of the few clothes it contained. It must be that textbook on navigation. She was glad to let Lau take it. Well, if navigation could be learned from a book, she would learn it! Could it be more difficult than Japanese or Kusaien, both of which she had been required to master? Surely some naval officer here at Kwajalein could give her a little help. She waved good-bye to the departing skiff and took one look at the *Star*. The schooner looked handsome and fit enough, when viewed from this safe distance. She had no thought of blaming her predecessor for the condition of the ship. Dr. Hanlin had taken over command, perforce, just as she had done. The ship had been badly battered when it arrived in the islands

after the long passage out from Boston. It had seen hard
service since then. Like herself, Dr. Hanlin had no way of
getting new parts swiftly when old ones wore out. The abil-
ities of Clement, the island engineer, were strictly limited.
And, she reflected, it is always harder for a man to make do
with little than it is for a woman. Women have an instinct
for this fine art. Then this certainly *was* a woman's job.

She walked up to the road with Lau and Luckabudge
trailing behind. She smiled, remembering how in Japan it
was always the woman who walked behind the lordly male.
The very name for wife—oku san—meant "the one behind."
How startled Japanese women always were to have an American man open the door for them and wait for them to pre-
cede him into a room! They found it embarrassing, almost
shocking. She supposed because she was captain, she must
now walk ahead. Rank had always been strictly observed
among the islanders, and this had been intensified under
Japanese rule.

She hailed a "cow car," a remarkable contraption of uncertain origin that bumped over the roads of Kwajalein Island, all three miles of its length and the scant half mile
of its width. They got out at the commissary and from there
Lau and Luckabudge returned to the *Star* with several
weeks' supply of foodstuffs. Milk, sugar, and canned meat
should go far toward rebuilding the somewhat shattered
morale of her crew.

Eleanor's next call was at the Navy Administration Building. It was distinguished from the nearby Quonset huts by a
flagpole and a pair of cannons, a strip of grass some genius
had caused to grow, and by a half dozen small coconut trees.
She presented herself to the executive officer and asked to
see Captain Cecil Gill, then in command at Kwajalein. The
sight of a civilian lady, especially a gray-haired lady without
lipstick or other trace of make-up, made that officer suspect
she was *not* a Navy wife. Then *who* could she be? Civilians
did not belong here. Indeed, they were not permitted. His
eyebrows went up.

"I am Eleanor Wilson, the Protestant missionary from Majuro," she explained. "I would like to pay my respects to Captain Gill."

"Just a moment, please. I'll tell him you're here." Privately he wondered just how much time the commanding officer would take to talk to a lady missionary.

Eleanor's interview with the Captain was a brief one. He was a very busy man, she knew. He welcomed her aboard, in Navy parlance, and promised whatever help the busy Navy shops could give her. She thanked him and assured him of the Mission Board's appreciation. She next checked in at "Hell's Angels." This was service slang for the nurses, and during the war the name had also been applied to their quarters. These, however, were now dignified by the name of "Women Officers' Quarters." There she took a shower, put on a fresh dress and left her bag in the curtained cubicle assigned to her. She now had a roof over her head ashore, albeit a tin one that probably leaked! And here she had decent feminine privacy and a "head" that worked. She must go back and forth to the *Star,* but this would be her *pied à terre,* a thing for which every seaman longed.

It was blinding hot when she left the building. The sun was nearing the zenith. Noon already! She looked at the cheap little watch she had bought at the ship's store on Guam. It said 11:55. Her good watch had long since given up the ghost to the tropics.

Kwajalein was a small island, but it seemed to Eleanor today that its various services were located in widely separated spots. In this climate one could not walk even a short distance without fatigue. She wiped the perspiration from her glasses as she waited for another cow car to take her to the officers' mess for chow. Ladies were not supposed to perspire, but in this heat one could hardly call the moisture on one's body "glow." In a few moments her fresh crisp dress was damp, even across the shoulders where it showed so badly. She mopped her face with a large embroidered handkerchief that had been the gift of a parishioner.

The lunch was excellent—good American food. She ate it gratefully. It was hard to leave the relative coolness indoors for the stifling heat without, but she must.

Soon she was standing before the Port Captain explaining to that astonished gentleman that, as the only member of the American Mission Board left in the Marshall Islands, she was in full charge of the *Morning Star.* He stared at her for a moment in complete disbelief. Something in his manner, which even his customary politeness could not disguise, made her straighten her back.

"I will, of course, check in with you before leaving the lagoon. I assume that it is not necessary to have permission to sail inside the reef? I have a capable island captain who knows sailing by landmarks."

The Port Captain agreed that this was permissible. "Let me know if I can be of any service to you," he said. Eleanor knew this was real kindness, not mere formality.

Then she was outside once more in the pitiless sun. Oh, for a jeep! Every missionary should have a jeep. If she were ever rich, she vowed she would buy one for every mission station. She did get a ride to the Air Force Terminal. She watched the planes taking off from the cement runways. It was only a few minutes' flying time to islands, where a boat might fight for days against current and tide to make a landing. Maybe a mission ought to have it own plane, one that could land on the water, she thought. With these thoughts, she turned and entered the airport shop.

"I have come to get my chronometer," she said in her most businesslike voice. "I am Miss Wilson of the *Morning Star.*"

The young airman grinned at her. "I heard about you, ma'am! So you're the new skipper! Glad I'm not in your shoes! These are the toughest seas in the world to sail. About your chronometer, ma'am, you'd better leave it here for a while. We've been working on it, but it's just about no good. It gains one day and loses the next. You really need a new one."

Eleanor's brow furrowed. "But can't you regulate it as you would a clock?" she asked innocently.

The young man groaned. "We've tried, ma'am, but it won't stay fixed. It . . . it's as crazy as a loon! One day it gains forty seconds; the next day it loses twenty!"

"I . . . I couldn't do anything about it at sea?" Eleanor asked, hesitantly. You set a clock ahead if it is slow; you set it back if it is fast. Wasn't a chronometer a seagoing clock? Why should it be so different?

"Lady!" the young man explained. "Even if it was a *good* chronometer, you wouldn't dare touch it at sea. All chronometers gain or lose. You have it checked on land and then just keep track of the rate of loss or gain and allow for that when you take your shots. This thing's a gone goose. It's done for. In my opinion, you might as well use a dollar watch!"

"I have a watch that keeps good time," Eleanor said cheerfully. "It loses about forty seconds a day—regularly. They checked it for me at the Coast Guard Station near the mission. Why can't I just use it? Does a few seconds make such a difference?" Her query was so innocent that the young airman gasped.

"Lady," his tone was patient, "one second off the correct time will mean you'll be a quarter of a mile wrong in your position. Forty seconds, and you're ten miles wrong! It would make a whale of a difference when you're looking for an island the size of your hat!"

Eleanor sat down weakly on a bench. "That sort of knocks the bottom out of things," she said. "Even if I learn to use a sextant and to work out the ship's position, it won't be correct unless I have the right time, exact to the second."

"That's it, ma'am. But you can get the time tick several times a day from our station on your radio." This he felt sure would console her for the state of her chronometer.

Eleanor looked at him fixedly. "But our radio isn't working. Our generator was ruined by salt water. We have no electric power."

The young man whistled dolorously. "Jeepers!" he said, and for the moment could think of nothing more to say. Yet when she had gone, he muttered to himself, "I bet she'll make it somehow. There's something about these missionaries. They came here to do a job, and, by gad, they do it!" There was real admiration in his words. He wished he knew how to be of help to this indomitable little lady with the soft white hair. What a big task she'd bitten off!

He looked at the chronometer of the *Morning Star*. "Junk!" he said disgustedly. "Just plain junk!" It had been a very fine chronometer when the *Star* left Boston back in 1947, but it had been jolted and jarred in many a stormy gale since then. This was March, 1950.

Eleanor felt she could never have made it to the Boat Pool on foot. She "jumped" another cow car, and in it she rattled over the hard road. It reminded her somehow of a Black Maria, the horse-drawn patrol wagon of yesteryear. At the Boat Pool she faced a puzzled and regretful Navy technician, this time an engine mechanic.

"You mean the parts for that three-cylinder Grey Marine Diesel job, ma'am?" he asked. "Gosh, I'm sorry, but they haven't come. We could fix it, if we had them. Otherwise, it's just impossible."

The full and terrible gravity of the situation swept over Eleanor. Without an accurate chronometer they might sail by landmark and compass to nearby islands, but without an engine, how could they get through the passes in the reefs? This was the most dangerous part of sailing among coral atolls. Without power the most skillful sailor was at the mercy of wind and tide.

There was no way to expedite matters. She did not even know from what firm Dr. Hanlin had ordered the engine parts. She must, then do without an engine until they should come. They would just have to depend on sails. After all, the three earliest *Morning Stars* had had nothing else. They had done their work without auxiliary power. She shut from her conscious mind the memory of their fate.

"Where do I go to inquire about the new sails we have ordered from Honolulu?"

"To Shipping and Receiving. It's that oblong building down by the laundry. I hope you get your new sails, ma'am," he said fervently. "I'm afraid you're going to need 'em!"

When she had gone he shook his head over the future prospects of the schooner *Morning Star*.

Eleanor walked slowly but with determination to face the next obstacle in her path. The man on duty shook his head. He was quite impersonal about it, not realizing that he was delivering the final blow to her hopes. No, there was no package of any kind addressed to the mission. Was she sure the canvas had left Honolulu? She would do well to radio the firm from which it was ordered. It was pulling teeth, he added, for a civilian to get anything out here.

"Ma'am, if you got any top Navy connections, use 'em! That's the only way to get action. Try somebody you know at Pearl."

Eleanor thanked him. She had no "top connections" at Pearl. She was just one lady missionary alone on an atoll. The weight of the world was now on her shoulders. She looked at her watch with a kind of morbid interest in its accuracy. That life should depend on a matter of seconds! She set her lips. She would not give way to despair, certainly not here where people could see.

But what hope was there? Without a generator, the radio was useless; the chronometer was worthless; the engine could not be repaired for many weary weeks, if ever; and now the new canvas had not come. The sails aboard the *Morning Star* were like blankets on which the moths had spent a summer. They would be torn to shreds in the first hard blow! Unless she got new canvas, it would be madness to leave the lagoon of Kwajalein. No wonder the Port Captain had looked so dubious. Doubtless he had inspected the *Star* while Dr. Hanlin was in charge. He knew what she was up against.

It was late afternoon now and walking was becoming

really painful. She was picked up by a young Navy man in a jeep.

"Lady, you hadn't ought to be walkin' in this heat! Hop in," he said. "What's your port of debarkation?"

"The Woman Officers' Quarters," she said.

"Hell's Angels!" Then he added apologetically, "I ain't swearin', ma'am, honest. That's what they call the nurses and their quarters. Be better if they called it heaven! They're the only American women on the island, except the officers' wives. But we only get to look at the nurses!" he said regretfully. "They rate as officers. Still," he added philosophically, "that's better'n nothing. At least you don't forget what a white woman looks like. At least, some don't." He gave her a sidelong glance. Probably she would not understand what he left unsaid.

Eleanor understood much better than he supposed. Few civilians guess how much of life in the raw the clergymen, and particularly missionaries, see, nor the worldly wisdom their counseling entails. Island romances between servicemen and Marshallese girls did exist, but they were not too common. They usually ended in heartbreak. Even if the young man married the girl, he knew he could not take her home to the states without serious complications. Not only missionaries, but the Navy authorities did all they could to discourage such alliances. Both island girls and young Navy men had asked her for advice. It placed her in a difficult position. How could she explain to an island girl how unsuited she would be for life in the States, and how unhappy she would be there? Worse still, how could she explain the very touchy question of race relations to people who regarded Americans, especially Bostonians, as their brothers in Christ? Such alliances, temporary or permanent, had been a problem since the first Navy ship touched at the islands. No one blamed the lonely serviceman too severely, and who could blame a Marshallese girl for wishing to have a part in the fabulous world from which these young men came?

"I ain't gettin' into no mix-up, ma'am!" the Navy boy

said hastily. "I got a girl back home. Keeps a man straight, rememberin'. She writes to me every day. Sometimes I get three letters on one plane, but she writes one *every day*."

"That's fine," Eleanor said. "I hope you won't forget her."

A Marine was on duty at the desk of the women's quarters. "Ma'am," he said politely, "I was to tell you, you have to report in at night by eleven o'clock. It's regulations."

Eleanor smiled. "I think I can manage that," she said. Ordinarily this situation would have amused her, but right now she had no heart for humor. She made it to her curtained cubicle, pulled the curtain shut, and dropped down on the cot. She was utterly spent. Not even the noisy radio at the other end of the building disturbed her. She did not really hear it. For the moment, she was shutting out the world. From somewhere within herself she was drawing strength to surmount the difficulties which lay across her path.

CHAPTER VI

The Open Sea

SIX WEEKS ASHORE proved beyond question to Eleanor that the Navy men had been all too right about her equipment. The chronometer refused all attempts at regulation; the generator that once powered the radio had gone into the discard; the engine was now at the Boat Pool waiting for the final parts to arrive. Nor had her appeals brought canvas for new sails from Honolulu. It was perhaps the stubborn Connecticut Yankee strain in Eleanor Wilson that responded with amazing equanimity to these handicaps, once the finality of them had struck home.

The lay mind might not follow her train of thought, nor have arrived at the same conclusion. But a missionary must have a philosophy made of sterner stuff. The *Star* must be sailed to the outlying islands. The work of the Lord required it. She must go to Jabwor, on Jaluit Atoll, to build a shelter house for workers, so that the people could go back to their devastated land to plant coconuts and breadfruit. Not all the bombing had been at Kwajalein. She had the lumber and roofing salvaged from old Navy buildings. She could get workers on Jaluit, but she must provide transportation for them. Therefore, they must sail, and at once.

The mission on Jabwor was now only a ruin. It must be rebuilt. This work she owed to the memory of Carl Heine, the Australian missionary, who had lived and worked there.

The schooner's hull was sound. It would be easy sailing to Jaluit Atoll, straight down the Sunset Chain of the Marshall Islands. They need never be long out of sight of land on a single course to the southeast. They had made several trips inside the lagoon, and Eleanor was convinced of the seaworthiness of the *Star* and of the ability of her seamen. Besides, she had spent every leisure moment studying Mixter's *Primer of Navigation.* "Primer" seemed to her an ironical term for that book, for it was complex enough to a raw beginner. Mathematics had never been her forte. Her mind was used to linguistic and theological studies, which had developed quite other faculties than those required of a navigator. She decided it was useless to concentrate on lighthouses and buoys. There were none, or none to speak of, in all her sea-borne parish of isles. What she needed was to get her position at sea by the stars.

Faithfully she wrote out the rules and committed them to memory. She worked out the problems given in the book. The steps were clear. First, you got the altitude of a star with the sextant. She could soon pick out the principal navigation stars from the chart. There are only twenty first-brightness stars in both hemispheres, and many of them were not visible in the islands, eight degrees above the equator. It boiled down to about a half-dozen she needed to know at this season. She picked them out on every clear night until they were as familiar to her as landmarks on the earth. A thrill of pleasure came over her. It was as if she had never really appreciated the beauty of the starry sky before. It had been little more than a background for her thoughts of celestial worlds. The heavens had been a matter of spiritual rather than temporal importance. Now it was both, and it took on an added luster. As Eleanor walked the strip of beach near her quarters, well before the curfew hour of eleven, she knew that life for her had taken on a new dimension. Why was not astronomy a required subject in every school? Surely, it gave the student a perspective he could get nowhere else.

So the stars were now her friends. She watched the waves on the shore, but the thought of trusting them as sailing guides seemed too impractical. The ancient Polynesian navigators, seeking new islands as increased population threatened their limited food supply, might have developed a sixth sense so that they could steer by wave patterns. She knew that as one approached an island the pattern of the waves grew smaller. As one left the shelter of land, it grew larger. There were spots in the ocean where two currents met, where the color of the water was typical of one spot—to a hawk-eyed island captain. Certain birds and fish were seen only at specific times of the year in definite regions of the sea and within known radii of land. Cloud masses tended to form over islands, especially over high islands. Refraction of light made the islands themselves sometimes appear higher than the level of the sea. All these things helped.

But the hard facts of navigation remained. Back in 1936, a native sailing boat set out from Jaluit for Ebon Island, which lay to the southwest. It was long believed lost, when it appeared off Kusaie, in the Caroline Islands, four hundred miles due west of its starting point. Aboard it had been a Marshallese girl who had attended school on this high island. The others had never been out of the Marshalls before, and so had never seen a high island. They mistook craggy Kusaie off in the distance for a terrible black cloud. The mission girl cried, "We are saved! Those are the high mountains of Kusaie!"

In 1949 another craft with an island "navigator" aboard had set out from Jaluit for Ailinglaplap, northwest up the Sunset Chain. It went so far off course, it by-passed the atoll entirely and ended up at Kwajalein.

Eleanor began to wonder if long ago navigation in these islands had not been to a large extent a matter of trial and error. Time meaning nothing, and food consisting of coconut meat and milk, a small crew could exist for weeks until a landfall was finally made. The islanders were inured to subsisting for long periods on scant food and little water.

She recalled Dr. Emory, the famous ethnologist of Bishop Museum, Honolulu, saying that perhaps only one canoe in a thousand of the early voyages ever made land. The rest perished at sea. The islanders believed that their bones had been swallowed up by the Giant Tridacna, the magical giant clam of legend. Eleanor had no notion of leaving her bones or the bones of her crew for this fabled monster; not if by diligent study she could work out her star sights and get a position at sea.

The principle was this: You took your star sight and made a few corrections from the *Nautical Almanac*. You knew your approximate latitude and longitude. If you didn't, you had to assume them. Your sight would correct your error.

That wonderful *Nautical Almanac* with the bright yellow cover was the most amazing secular book Eleanor Wilson had ever had occasion to use. It gave the position of every important heavenly body—sun, moon, planets, and stars— for every second of the year. If the star had swung one hundred degrees past the Meridian of Greenwich and you knew where you were in longitude from that magic line, ergo, you knew the Local Hour Angle of that star—its angular distance from you—at the second you made your shot.

The rest was mechanical. It took drill to be quick and to avoid errors, but soon Eleanor found she could run down a shot in a very few minutes. She soon learned how to use the tables. The H.O. No. 214 (U.S. Hydrographic Office Publication No. 214) was quite a set of books, one for each ten degrees of latitude. Luckily the *Star* had these. The latitude, the position of the sun or star above or below the equator, and its local hour angle were the three things one needed. From then on, it was like looking up a name in the telephone directory.

The answer, with one correction, gave the true altitude of the star from the supposed position of your ship and its bearing. The difference between this altitude and the corrected sextant reading told you how many miles you were toward that body, or away from it, along that bearing. How the tables knew all this was like other great mysteries inexplicable to mortals, or so Eleanor thought. She did not turn

Calvinist and question the nature of things. For this once, she merely accepted and asked no questions.

She was just at the point of attempting to put this information on the chart, when a young Navy officer came aboard the *Star*. He looked at her quizzically.

"Need a little help?" he asked.

"Hello, Lieutenant Dodd! Indeed, I do. You have come just in time. Show me how to put my last night's star shots on the chart."

He looked at her work. "You've got your intercepts and your bearings. The rest's a cinch."

He took her parallel rulers and dividers and showed her how to put the ruler at the right bearing on the compass rose and walk it across the chart to run that line through the ship's supposed position. Along this he measured the distance toward one star and away from another. From these he drew two lines that crossed, giving a "fix," or the exact position of the ship. It was so easy when one knew how! He could stay only a few moments, so there was no chance to ask how to plot a course in advance so one would know what compass course to steer. To learn this, one Saturday afternoon she sought out her friend, Perez, a young Air Force navigator.

"Here I am for help," she said. "Would you have time to show me how to lay out a course?"

"I sure have. I'm off duty this afternoon."

He spread the large scale chart of the Marshall Islands on his desk. The islands lay in two parallel chains, running northwest to southeast. She immediately picked out Kwajalein in the western or Sunset Chain and her "home port" of Majuro in the southern end of the Sunrise Chain. Its direction from Kwajalein was southeast by east. It was no trick at all to see what course one ought to steer to go directly from Kwajalein to Majuro. Of course, there was the matter of wind and current, but at the moment Eleanor was thinking only of the compass course and praying for a fair and following wind.

"Now I must plan the course from Kwajalein to Jaluit. That's almost straight southeast right down the Sunset Chain. We hope to leave here for Jaluit on the twenty-eighth of this month."

Perez looked up quickly. "Say, are you really going to Jaluit so soon?" he asked eagerly.

"Yes. I want to be there when the delegation from the United Nations arrives. Do you want a ride?" Eleanor could not help smiling. A month ago none of the Navy personnel would have ventured outside the harbor on the *Star!*

Perez grinned. "Not exactly. I expect I'll be navigator on the plane with the V.I.P.'s. Do you think you could put down a buoy for us at Imroij Island in Jaluit Atoll? That's where our plane has to land. Every time we throw out an anchor at Imroij, we lose it. It would be a big help if our planes could tie up there to a floating buoy."

Eleanor considered. "We'd like to help, of course, if we're able. How heavy is it?"

"Not too heavy for the *Morning Star,* even with the cable and the anchor. I'll have to speak to the C.O., but I know he'll be delighted if you can do it. We'll put it aboard the *Star,* and all you need do is just heave it over the side when you get there."

"We'll be glad to do that." Like all good New Englanders she liked to repay an obligation. "Count on us!"

"That's swell, Miss Wilson. You just pull up to the pier on the morning of the twenty-eighth, and we'll get it aboard."

The morning of April twenty-eighth was hot and clear. The *Star* lay at her anchorage off Emon Beach. The schooner glistened with a new coat of paint, and the sun glanced off her brightwork. Even the men's clothes were spotless. Aboard ship the odor of soap and water was a big improvement over that of dirt, grime, and sweat. Apparently if one wanted to have a clean ship, one must be something of a martinet. What Eleanor did not realize was that she had no first mate. It was the first mate's job to handle the men and turn out the work. The bo'sun was his foreman to execute the job—a kind of merchant marine equivalent of the Army "Top Kick" and the Navy Chief. Without such an officer, the armed services and the captains of merchant vessels had long since learned that there was little accomplished. Some curious thing in men's make-up made it seem childish to work, if they were not driven to it. They feared being accused by their fellows of apple-polishing.

Well, they were ready to leave. This was the Rubicon, and the die was cast! She stowed the chronometer, useless as it was, back in the cabin. The dead engine was ashore, the dead generator had been sent to Davy Jones' locker. The old sails had been mended. There were no new ones. The dinghy was hoisted aboard and made secure on deck. All the men but Anliri were at the windlass, hauling in the anchor. The blue life jackets lay on the deck where they had been thrown, and the glass water jars stood in a row just as they had been placed as they were brought from shore. Eleanor threw an old piece of canvas over them. Where had she read that a water jar could act like a burning glass and set a ship afire? It was curious how many bits of sea lore came back to her, their source forgotten. As soon as they were under way, she told Freddy to secure the water bottles, stow the life jackets in the chest where they belonged, and to order a man to stand by to heave the white canvas fenders over the side as they approached the Navy pier.

There was something in Eleanor's manner that made the crewmen study her out of the corners of their eyes. She walked with a new assurance, a new confidence, which was not assumed. It came from the inner conviction that she had a job to do and that she had fitted herself for it as best she could. The rest was now in the Lord's hands.

"I hope the buoy is at pier ready to be put aboard," she said.

"Yes, Mother Wilson," Anliri answered without enthusiasm. He did not want to go on this trip. He had been so sure he would not have to! Now he could not refuse without losing face, so go he must. Anliri had had no experience in laying buoys and was not anxious to acquire any. Mother Wilson, however, had made up her mind, and she *was* the captain. A woman! The old island mariner shrugged. Even in the Marshalls where the male was still the dominant sex, men knew it was useless to argue with a woman when she had made up her mind.

There were many curious glances as they tied up to the pier. A Navy truck was waiting with a crew of men to put the buoy aboard. It was a black and yellow rubber "doughnut" perhaps a yard in diameter. It looked too small to hold a plane, but, of course, it was the anchor and cable attached to it that did the work. It took only a few moments to load these aboard.

Eleanor then checked in with the young lieutenant at the Port Office. "We're leaving for Jaluit this morning," she told him smiling. Then she added, not too seriously, "And if you don't hear from us in two weeks, send out a search party."

"I won't wait that long!" Lieutenant Dauzat said.

It was a rather big decision to make—to leave Kwajalein Atoll. But the hull was sound, and the sails should do at this season for a two-hundred-mile run. It was southeast all the way, and they could skirt the islands of the Sunset Chain. Anliri had sailed to Namu and Ailinglaplap. Jaluit was just another day's sail to the southeast. They should make it in two days and two nights, with luck. Indeed, if they were to be there to greet the delegation from the United Nations, they must have favorable winds all the way.

They were ready to sail now and all the crew were aboard except one new deck hand, Bolej. He had promised to be here waiting for them. They were late already. When they had waited fifteen minutes for him, Eleanor called Anliri. There was a grim set to her chin. She would not be delayed a moment longer. She felt that if they did not start at once, something untoward might happen and the voyage would never be completed.

"Anliri, can you manage without another man—without Bolej?"

From his seat in the cockpit Anliri tilted up his small head to look at her. He studied the wind with the weatherwise look of an old seaman. Then he nodded.

"Yes, Mother Wilson. Not bad winds this time of year. We can manage, if it does not blow too hard."

"Very well then. Shove off!"

Anliri called out a few words in Marshallese. The jib was hoisted to pull them away from the pier. Then the fores'le, stays'le and mains'le were shaken out. They caught a bit of the offshore breeze and, slowly but with growing momentum, *Morning Star VI* moved out into the lagoon. Eleanor looked at her watch. It was just past noon. The *Star* quivered now as her sails filled. Anliri swung her on the starboard tack and headed for South Pass.

Eleanor could scarcely believe they were really under way —and bound for Jaluit.

Then a shout was raised by Luckabudge. "There's Bolej! Bolej is at the pier."

"We will not go back for him," Eleanor said firmly. Then she was startled to see Bolej leap aboard a Navy M Boat which headed for them, throwing up a bow wave of white spray. Anliri slackened sail. Over went the fenders once more. Bolej, sure-footed, as all his people were, leaped laughing from the M Boat to the deck of the *Star*. He dropped his "luggage" to the deck. It was a furoshiki bundle—all his worldly goods tied up, Japanese fashion, in a colored cotton handkerchief. He waved back to the Navy crew.

"Yokwe Kom!" he called. There was more, but that was all his Navy friends could understand.

Post pier head jump, making the boat after it has left the pier, Eleanor thought. She looked severely at Bolej. She was about to berate him soundly, when suddenly she repented. He stood with his head hanging, a picture of guilt and contrition. It was as if a dog had come with a slipper in his mouth, saying mutely, "Beat me!"

"I am sorry, Mother Wilson. My laundry wasn't ready!"

What could she say?

All sails were hoisted now and sheeted home. The wind was freshening and it was from the northwest. That was about as favorable a wind as they could expect. The *Star* made for the South Pass as if she had taken a bone in her teeth.

"She's glad to go, glad to go!" Eleanor told herself exultantly. "She knows she can do it. She isn't afraid."

CHAPTER VII

Mission Accomplished

"SOUTHEAST TO JALUIT!"

It was like a song the wind sang in the rigging as the *Morning Star VI* plunged her slender bow into the Pacific. As they neared South Pass, the crew became alert. Luckabudge climbed into the rigging, Boaz stood watch at the forepeak, the others by either rail. The Pass, too narrow for large ships, was wide enough for the *Star*. Still they must use all care. Anliri was at the helm. What a blessing that the wind was from the northeast! It would blow them directly through the Pass!

The danger of green water that marked the coral ledge was so familiar that islanders had forgotten their fear of it. Boats went aground, but not often, and in every island mariner was some inborn feeling that such mischance would not happen to him. Had he dwelt upon this peril, his way of life would have been intolerable. So Anliri steered with confidence, and soon they were out of the pass. He peered ahead, trying to pierce the gray-green line of the distant horizon to the southeast, as if with his telescopic sight he might catch a glimpse of Namu Atoll, thirty miles away. With this wind they should be making four knots. It would be nine in the evening before Namu lay broad abeam. They would keep well to the west of the atoll, for there were no shore lights to warn them off. Anliri drew a deep breath— they were over deep water now and on a course he knew well, to Namu and Ailinglaplap, with Jaluit just beyond.

No need now for all hands to keep sharp watch. He raised a call. The words were indistinguishable, but the response was instantaneous. Down from the rigging came Luckabudge. Boaz stopped his intent scrutiny of the water from the fore-peak, where he had lain prone, peering below. A sense of ease, of sheer luxurious content came over the crew. The moment of tension past, it was promptly forgotten. No wonder, Eleanor thought, that such a thing as a "nervous break-down" was unknown to the Marshallese. The islanders knew something the American and European had forgotten—how to let nature heal fatigue. If anyone was "on watch" now, it was not apparent to the casual eye.

The Marshallese language had words for all things neces-sary to island living—in short, for fishing, for building houses and canoes, and for making love. This was all that had been necessary until the Modern Age came with the ships of Spaniard, of pirate, of German, Japanese, and Amer-ican. Therefore, when other words were necessary, they were borrowed from the outlander. "Gun" they learned when their warriors fell dead on the beach with no spear thrust through their bodies. "Chair" and "table" and "bunk" came over intact from English; also the Japanese words "undoba" (athletic field), "dempo" (radiogram), and "toban" (the man on watch). It was only five years since their Japanese masters had been driven off and they had learned English, or its American equivalent, from the young men of the Navy and the Marines. Yet many Japanese terms lingered aboard ship.

Eleanor looked anxiously about at the crew. They were lounging about the deck, happy as a family on an outing. Lau, seated on the deck, was slicing potatoes for the evening meal. Beside him was a bucket of salt water for washing them. Even Anliri sat behind the wheel as relaxed as a cat, apparently dreaming of other voyages in other days. It was too much for the New England psyche.

Eleanor rose and walked with purposeful step toward the compass. Always praise when you could. That was the first and vital rule of a missionary. She saw with pleasure that the course was just as she had set it, hovering about 164 degrees. She looked at Anliri with real pleasure.

"You steer a very good course, Anliri," she said warmly. "And all the time I thought you were steering by landmarks!"

Anliri looked blank. He had been! How else, when one was but a half-hour out of his familiar "home port"? But he was too polite to contradict a lady minister of the gospel.

"Yes, Mother Wilson," he agreed with some enthusiasm. "One hundred and sixty-four degrees. Maybe the compass needle swing a little to 162 or maybe a little to 166, but it stays very close to 164, just like you said." He said this as if the credit were all hers. This was the customary island politeness! Eleanor felt a little foolish. He had not once glanced at the compass. She had been watching him intently.

"Be sure to tell the man who relieves you to do the same," she said. "They are not all like you, Anliri! I think you have a little compass inside you that tells you how to steer! They say the birds have just that, something inside them that guides them on their long journeys."

Anliri grinned. "Maybe so, Mother Wilson. My grandfather, his grandfather, and his grandfather, they sailed these waters. They teach me by quiet words inside me which way to go, what way to sail, where is the land!"

This did not startle a Micronesian missionary. It was no uncommon thing for a native to say his grandfather or great-grandfather had taught him some art necessary to his life, even if that progenitor had died before the speaker was born. Was there a continuous flow of race consciousness that islanders knew and understood, some secret source of knowledge to which they were attuned? Had they some means other than books by which to pass on the lore of one generation to another? Sometimes Eleanor felt that they had. For whatever reason, islanders were very reluctant to tell anything of their past history, as they believed it would bring them bad luck.

"I am sure there is a great deal in inheritance, Anliri," Eleanor said. "But we must make use of knowledge from books as well. The books were written by men who sailed the sea and passed on to us the learning of their grandfathers and great-grandfathers."

This was a new thought to the island captain. He nodded gravely.

"Yes," he said, "the grandfathers of the Americans were great sailors. When they came here to hunt the whale, our people wondered at their great ships. On my island we have a harpoon that a whaleman gave my ancestors because they cared for him when he was sick. The people of his ship sailed away and left him."

Eleanor flushed. She knew only too well the harsh practice of old-time sailing masters. It was perhaps dictated by necessity but by any moral standard it was indefensible. The sick were put ashore to die; often they spread sickness among the islanders who, out of humanity, cared for them. Small pox had decimated the Indians of New England before the landing of the Pilgrim Fathers. Presumably the disease had been contracted by the Indians in the same fashion as in the Pacific Islands—from marooned seamen set ashore. Whole settlements had been wiped out. She recalled with a sense of horror how an historian of the time had called this "the merciful Providence of God"! Anliri was too courteous to say whether or not the sailor his kinsmen had cared for had spread death among the people.

There was a sharp shift in the wind. It was blowing now from the west.

"Babwe!" The cry was raised simultaneously by captain and crew. Instantly Anliri headed to starboard. The schooner responded like a horse to the touch of the rein.

"Babwe means starboard then or to the right," Eleanor said. "I meant to ask you so that we will understand each other."

"Yes," Anliri said with the air of a patient teacher. "Now babwe is to the right."

"Sometimes I have heard the men calling 'Kabwe.' That must mean to port or to the left." There was a veiled question in Eleanor's voice. It seemed simple but past experience in translating Marshallese into English had made her wary.

Anliri shook his head. "It is not always so. Sometimes the wind is the other way."

Slowly light dawned on the apprentice captain of the ship. The wind was now from the right or starboard. They were sailing "babwe" into it.

"Oh, I see. You don't use left and right at all! Babwe means into the wind and kabwe means away from the wind no matter from which direction it happens to be blowing."

"Of course! How else can a ship sail, but into the wind or away from the wind?" Anliri was not a linguist. It was hard to think that other people expressed themselves in any way but his.

Spray dashed over the bow. Eleanor ducked instinctively. Then she thought how foolish that was. The sea was warm and the air was mild. What harm could the spray do? She would take it in the face as one did in a canoe on the lagoon. She walked across the deck and seated herself in the cockpit. The sailing by daylight could be left safely to Anliri. She would prepare her Bible lesson. She did not miss the look of relief on the faces of the crewmen. The Bible was her business! The ship was theirs.

The sun was lowering in the west. They would have a glorious sunset and the sky promised fair weather for to-morrow. Luckabudge said so. They ate early—it was so much easier eating by daylight. With the generator gone, they had only kerosene running lights and a lantern or two for emergencies. For supper they had neither breadfruit nor coconuts, for barren Kwajalein produced no crops. Tonight, to save their rice, they had commissary potatoes, with canned corned beef, and tea. The tea was lukewarm, but it *was* tea. Lau could not understand that Americans preferred their food and drink hot. The islanders cared little whether their food was hot or cold. To them drinking tea was just a good excuse to empty the sugar bowl. They finished eating as the sun dipped below the horizon; the first rays of sunset began to color the sea. The crew of the *Star* seemed to have not a care in the world. Even Eleanor relaxed. If only the sunset could go on forever!

But there are no long twilights in the tropics. In the mid-latitudes where the sun rises and sets obliquely, there is a long interval between daylight and darkness. The far north and the far south have long twilights in their summer seasons. But here along the equator, the sun sets almost vertically, and night settles down with astounding rapidity. Eleanor was used to this, but with the darkness an old worry returned. By daylight, her crew had kept on course by landmarks. But would they keep on it after dark? Would they bother to use the flashlight to see the compass card? In her heart, she rather doubted it.

With some excitement she watched for the first evening star. She could not dash down the ladder two steps at a time like the sure-footed islanders, so she sent Freddy for her sextant well ahead of time. She went down just before it was dark enough to take her shots and checked her watch against the chronometer. Useless or not, she had put it back in its niche, where it was supposed to be safe against the rolling of the ship. It might not be accurate but this once it seemed to have lost the right number of seconds since yesterday—if her watch was holding to its regular rate of loss. She took the stop watch from its box, and the sheet she had ruled in advance to record times and altitudes. She watched eagerly for a star. Long before she could see one, Anliri was pointing. Freddy, anxious not to be roped in on this performance, made out that he could not see a single star. Eleanor smiled. She knew he had keen eyesight. It was necessary to be ready when first darkness fell, for to get good star shots one must have a clear horizon. If she waited too long, until the stars were bright, the horizon would be obscured and the sight would be inaccurate.

The crew watched with curiosity this spectacle of their lady skipper, legs astride, bracing herself on the deck against the roll of the ship, as she prepared to take her first shot. How, they thought, could a woman do a man's work? There was something not quite respectable about it, and respectability was something to be reckoned with in ironclad island custom.

High over head Pollux, in the constellation of the Twins, pierced the sky so clearly that even book-bred eyes could see it. Eleanor got the star in her sextant telescope and, moving the arm carefully, brought the reflection of the star down until it sat neatly on the horizon. Then she clicked her watch and set down the time and the altitude of the star. One shot recorded! It was so different, somehow so much more logical, to do this at sea than from the beach. A few moments later and Rigel, in Orion's foot, was out and well placed for observation. When she had Rigel on the now dimming horizon, she recorded the time and altitude. She saw Freddy watching.

"Here, Freddy, I want you to take a star sight before the light fades. It is really no more difficult than a sun shot when you get used to it." Freddy came reluctantly. The others would make fun of him if he did not do it as well as a woman. It would be insupportable to his pride. He tried to see the star, but could not. He shook his head in disgust.

"I can't see it," he said a little sulkily. Eleanor took the instrument and set the arm at the angle that brought the star exactly down to the horizon.

"Now, hold the telescope level, and it's right there."

Freddy's face brightened. "I see it! I see the star right on the edge of the sea!" He was all enthusiasm. He got the second star shot unaided, and thereupon gave himself airs when he was with the crewmen.

"It is nothing," he said deprecatingly. "How could it be

when even a woman can do it?" That settled the matter, of course.

But Eleanor knew they did not really believe in her ability to navigate. They would have to be shown. When she had gone below to work out her sights, Anliri smiled indulgently.

"We do not need the stars to tell us where we are! We know!" By wind and wave and common sense, in a manner of speaking, Anliri did. But what would he do if they were days out of sight of land and had been blown about in all directions by the four winds? But this was a possibility unnecessary to face today. To Anliri, worrying about the future was an unknown experience. He lived only in the moment. He knew he was sailing straight down the Sunset Chain for Namu and Ailinglaplap or Big Island, just beyond. Keeping a safe distance from the land on his left hand, he would make it to Jaluit, sailing "babwe" or "kabwe" according to the wind. He was content.

That was more than could be said of the lady navigator. Down in her cabin she was, in Navy parlance, "sweating it out." Just as she had done so successfully on land, she took her computations and consulted the miraculous book called "H. O. No. 214." She got her intercepts and bearings and plotted her position on the chart.

"No, no, it couldn't be!" According to these figures, she was off the coast of southern France! "I've failed," she thought weakly. "Now that I'm at sea, I can't really do it. On shore, it was just an exercise in the book. Now it's for real." Then reason asserted itself. She had done something wrong. She must find out what it was, or else admit it was too much for a woman, and let the men steer by wave patterns and the birds.

Suddenly she realized that in her excitement she had forgotten to change local time to Greenwich time—a mere matter of eleven hours' difference! They were in time zone minus eleven, or eleven east. They were eleven hours ahead of Greenwich time! How could she have made such an error? A correction of eleven hours meant a difference in longitude of eleven time zones, or nearly halfway around the earth.

With this correction swiftly made, she came out at longitude one hundred and sixty-eight degrees east; latitude eight degrees north. She was in the Marshall Islands, south of Kwajalein and right opposite Namu Atoll! It was all she could do to repress a shout of triumph. Missionaries are human after all! She ran up on deck. At the ladder head, she heard the shout.

"Namu! Namu, Mother Wilson!" All the crew had seen the faint dark line of a land mass to port.

Eleanor sat a long time on deck, watching the long, dark line of scattered islets that formed the broken chain of Namu Atoll.

Anliri was pleased. "And that's just where the star shots placed us, Anliri," she exclaimed. "Right off Namu Atoll. It worked! It worked!"

Freddy stole below and looked at the chart while she was topside. "It's true," he said. "Not that Mother Wilson would tell a lie! But she did come out right where we are. We saw Namu!"

He looked at the sextant box with awe. That box and that flat black book knew where everyone was on the face of the earth. Marvelous! From now on he would practice regularly. It would give him added prestige among the men.

On deck, Eleanor looked about regretfully. How she would love to sleep topside. But the men spread their blankets right here around the cockpit. She knew they would be shocked. Conventions here were more rigid in such matters than on Beacon Hill; and the fantail head was in close proximity. Still, in calm weather, the men stood in the net below the bowsprit.

It was hard for her to think of going below into that stuffy cabin. Here there was a breeze, and there was something hypnotic about watching the sea and looking up at the stars. How friendly they seemed—God's lighthouses set in the sky to guide his children. A strange sense of well-being came over her. Her tense nerves relaxed. Her body was at ease, her mind at rest. She was growing drowsy. She went below. She would sleep well tonight even if the cabin were hot. All was well aboard the *Morning Star*.

But the next day the sea roughened, and all day long as they skirted Ailinglaplap the spray from the salt-heavy Pacific deluged them. Their skins began to burn, but they dared not use fresh water to wash, for their water tanks were small and could not hold enough for both drinking and washing. And with no engine, if the wind failed, the *Star* might be becalmed for days. Washing with fresh water was a luxury they could not afford. Nothing had irked Eleanor in her long years of missionary service so much as the inability to keep clean at all times. Her neck burned, and she felt hot and sticky. By afternoon her dress clung dankly to her back. What wouldn't she give for a good cold shower with clean, sweet water before changing her clothes? She lay down on her bunk as always, fully dressed, and tried to use mental control on a purely physical state of discomfort.

It would take them most of the day to pass the long atoll of Ailinglaplap, meaning "big island" in Marshallese. It was no trouble to keep on course by day, for this island chain was their halfway marker on the trip to Jaluit. This, at least, was comforting. Eleanor must have fallen into a fitful sleep. She was rudely awakened by a crash overhead. Someone had slammed her skylight shut. Then she heard the blessed sound of rain, the violent rain of the tropics. A few drops splashed to the cabin floor. A miracle! This sudden tropical downpour would cool things off, but only on deck. It would take a polar wind to cool her breathless cabin. She jumped up. She must get wet. Her skin was burning. She was almost feverish. There on a hook hung her black bathing suit, which had been the object of a desperate search through the shops of Boston—a bathing suit suitable for a dignified lady missionary. The very thing! Eleanor was in it in a moment, snatched up her soap and towel, and was up the ladder with a speed that astonished her.

At first the blessed relief of being wet with clean, sweet water blotted out all else. Then she heard gasps of horror. The crew, stripped to small underpants, fled as far forward as they could without tumbling into the sea. She had forgotten the mores of Micronesia! Only the embarrassed helmsman clung to the wheel for physical and moral support, and he raised his eyes in mute appeal for help in this embarrassing dilemma.

How provoking! She glanced to see who was steersman. Bolej, fat, jolly Bolej who looked like a Buddha! He was enjoying the rain. Rivulets ran off his plump face and bare chest. And he had on dungarees! Apparently shorts were too unconventional for him to wear when he came aft!

Luckabudge was pulling the canvas cover over the dinghy. He never turned his head as he spoke.

"Mother Wilson, you better get inside. Bad shower. You will get wet!" There was urgency in his tone.

But Eleanor was adamant. "That's just what I'm hoping for! I shall perish if I cannot get clean."

Luckabudge turned and for the first time saw her in this unconventional garb. Unconventional! It had an adequate top and a full skirt falling to the knee. In cut it was a 1920 model. Odd that in the days of the Bikini suit it should so startle the natives of the very islands among which Bikini lay. Luckabudge looked as if he had seen a ghost in a graveyard. His eyes were like saucers. His jaw dropped. So did the coil of rope in his hand. It made a thud on the wet deck. Then he turned and ran for his life, forward where the crew were soaping themselves and enjoying the luxury of a bath.

Eleanor tugged at her skirt as if to pull it to her ankles. Well, it wouldn't go, and she wasn't going to miss this glorious opportunity. She soaped her arms and face and neck, and the soapsuds ran down her body and with them came the blessed comfort of cool cleanliness. It seemed impossible that a few moments before she had been close to agony from salt water burn. This was living again. Soap and rinse, soap and rinse, over and over. Oh, wasn't it good to be cool and clean! She tried not to glance forward, but she could hear the men's shouts. She heard the slap of wet cloth on still wetter wood. They would be soaping and washing their clothes. Such a chance as this did not come often. Their backs were as resolutely turned to her as hers to them. Plainly they were aghast at the idea of a missionary in a bathing suit. Even a proper Bostonian outmoded bathing suit was something of a sensation. She wiped the soapsuds from her face and stood, just letting the rain from heaven soak into her parched body. She knew just how a frog must feel when sitting in a puddle drinking through its skin.

She chuckled at the men's foolish attitude, and yet, she reflected, it would scarcely be believed at home, how strict the standards of the Micronesian people were. Over-romanticized tales of the South Seas had created a very false picture of island life. Only the Polynesian women and those of islands like Yap and Puluwat commonly went bare to the waist, a thing considered proper in their culture. Other islanders, even the men, felt it improper to appear before foreigners without shirts. Aboard ship, when she was present, it was rare for the crew to come aft in only shorts or dungarees. The first missionaries had brought with them the mores of the Victorian Era, and these remained long after the good old Queen had been laid to rest.

Well, she was cool, and that was the main thing. She was sorry to astonish her crewmen, but only a man in chains would have stayed in that cabin when there was a chance to come on deck and get wet! With all the dignity and sangfroid she could muster, she walked slowly to the ladder. She glanced at Bolej.

"Isn't it blessed to be cool again!" she remarked.

But Bolej flushed under his golden brown skin and, Buddha-like, continued to stare off to starboard. His answering mumble meant nothing in either Marshallese or in English. In his experience adults always went fully clothed into the sea to bathe. Eleanor smiled. Fully dressed for native women meant a faded, clinging cotton dress and a negligible amount of underwear. These were much more revealing than a lastex bathing suit. Oh, well. . . .

By five o'clock the decks of the *Star* were dry as well as clean. They were sailing along in the mellow evening light. The men were eating far forward while she sat in the cockpit near the helmsman. She finished eating and set down her dish.

"I'll take the wheel now, Boaz," she said, "so you can go forward and get your supper." Reluctantly he relinquished the helm.

"I can wait," he said.

"Oh, no, go and eat. I like to steer." This gave her an ideal chance to check their compass course. She had hardly had five minutes of feeling the helm in her hand, when Luckabudge came quickly aft and all but took it from her. He was firm, if deferential.

"But you have not had time to finish your supper," she objected.

"I have had enough," he said, with dignity. "It is not fitting that you should steer. It is not *woman's* work!" Even the faithful Luckabudge had reached the limit of what he could endure from the Atomic Age. Eleanor knew it was time to beat a strategic retreat. The respect of her crew for her as a seaman must come with time and experience. Well, they would be at Jaluit tomorrow. This would be the day the plane would arrive there with the United Nations delegates and distinguished visitors. They must not be late. They must get that buoy into the water before they heard the hum of the plane's motors.

They sighted Jaluit at a few minutes after five o'clock the following afternoon, April thirtieth. Darkness settled down more quickly than they could have wished. There was a good pass through the reef at Imroij, the South West Pass of the atoll, but unluckily in the darkness they were swept past it. When daylight came they were already far to the south of it and the wind had died down considerably. To beat back would have been difficult. It was easier to round the southern tip of the atoll and enter the lagoon from the east. But South East Pass was narrow and crooked, and, with the present direction of the wind, they were barred from entering it.

"We cannot make it!" Freddy the pessimist said with an air of authority.

"But we must make it!" Eleanor exclaimed. "We promised to lay that buoy!" They all looked at the huge black and yellow "doughnut" on their forward deck.

"Anliri," Eleanor asked anxiously, "can't we tack and get into the pass?" Her tone was pleading.

The grizzled old island seaman scanned the water and the shore. He seemed to be sniffing the wind, wondering if it would shift and give him a tiny margin of leeway. You can sail with the wind, you can tack and by skillful maneuvering sail several points into it, but there is a limit to what a boat propelled by wind power can do in narrow quarters such as the entrance to this pass.

"We will try," he said gravely.

He took the helm. A hand signal sent his crew to their places. There was a sense of a battle joined, the age-old conflict of men against the sea, men in whose veins ran the blood of a race that came out of Asia over the sea in frail canoes more than a thousand years ago.

Anliri tacked back and forth across the entrance to the pass, each time bringing the *Star* a few feet nearer to the open water of the lagoon. It was a demonstration of seamanship, Eleanor realized, that might make any yachtsman envious. It was not the work of the gilded amateur. It was the skill of a man who got his living from the sea, who neither scorned it nor could master it, but a man who had learned to live by its moods and its laws.

Time and again Eleanor drew in her breath. It took all her resolution to keep from crying out. The green water of the shallows was under their keel. What if the *Star* went aground? But she could do nothing. Only islanders would dare sail a ship so close to the jagged heads of coral. Just when disaster seemed imminent, Anliri called, "Riuk," meaning come about. The man far forward held the jib taut. The helm was thrown over and the great boom of the mainsail swung perilously overhead. They were off on the other tack, but always nearer and nearer their goal. Foot by foot in a zigzag pattern across the narrow pass they sailed. The coordination of these men would have made a crew in a Bermuda race envious. They moved to a rhythm all their own.

Then on the last tack, they made it! The *Star* crept between clutching jaws of coral into the wide and sheltered lagoon of Jaluit Atoll. A cheer went up from the men.

"Well done!" Eleanor cried. "Well done, Anliri! I am proud of you all!" She went up and shook the island captain's hand.

But even yet there were dangers, for this part of the lagoon was dotted with coral heads. Eleanor fretted inwardly. Would they ever get to the anchorage in time to lay that buoy? They were approaching Imroij, when the keen-eared crew began staring up into the blue. It was Luckabudge who first saw the plane. He had the famous telescopic sight of the Micronesian.

"The plane is coming! The plane is coming!" he shouted.

Only then was Eleanor aware of any sound, and it was still several minutes before she saw the sun glinting on its wings. It had come from Kwajalein in an hour and a half and they had been nearly three days on the way!

Despair gripped her. It was not her fault that they had missed the proper pass and wasted all this precious time, but she felt responsible. The roar of the plane's motors was louder now, and the plane was losing altitude. There was Imroij dead ahead. They would be too late—and only by a maddening few minutes. Hadn't Perez said all they needed to do was dump the buoy over the side? If only they could get there!

But the plane was not landing! It dipped a wing in token of recognition. They waved violently in return. Then the plane headed east. Eleanor grasped what it must be doing.

"They are taking the visitors to see the famous ruins at Jabwor eight miles away across the lagoon!" she exclaimed in delight. "That gives us time, just time. Anliri, can't you crowd on just a little more sail!"

The flight over Jabwor would indeed delay the plane, but what in the world did they hope to see? Jabwor had been the capital of the islands under both Germans and Japanese, but our bombers had used it as a target and there was literally nothing left of it, certainly not enough to be seen from the air. Then she understood. Perez must be aboard that plane. He had seen their dilemma and was giving them time.

Why wouldn't those sails fill? What was it they said of the old clipper ships that went around the Horn—that they had on all sail and the captain's shirt hanging from the main truck! If she had had one, she would have hung it there!

They were almost at the spot now, not far from the tiny rock pier at Imroij. The PBY had circled back and was gliding downward, making a graceful landing on the lagoon. The plane door opened and several heads popped out. The people smiled and waved to the chagrined company aboard the *Star*.

"We can't get it over in time," Freddy said.

"We can and we must!" Eleanor said sharply. It was her first absolute order except for giving the helmsman their course. "All of you, get forward and heave that thing over the rail!"

There was a rush for the starboard rail forward. Lines were cast off. The men gave a great heave. One, two, three, and the great rubber doughnut was over the rail. It plopped into the water like a baby whale that had been dumped into the ocean.

"Heave ho, my hearties!" Eleanor said under her breath. Someone released the anchor of the buoy just in time. It plummeted into the lagoon, causing the metal cable on deck to unwind. There was a harsh sound of metal biting into wood and the smell of burning varnish. The cable was gouging out the gunwale of the *Star!* Freddy and Lucka-budge, moving like lightning, seized a spar and thrust it between gunwale and wire coil.

And just in time. When the last inch of cable had gone over the side, Anliri called, "Jerok! Hoist sail!"

A cheer went up from the crew and passengers of the Navy plane. It taxied up to the float. The pilot was laughing like a boy, for all that there was top brass aboard his plane. Later she heard that Admiral Fiske had exclaimed, "I never saw a buoy laid that fast before!"

Aboard the *Star*, Eleanor smiled, well content. The *Star's* first mission had been a success. Her crew had been equal to its task. It was a good omen, a very good omen for the days to come.

CHAPTER VIII

Jabwor Revisited

THE UNITED NATIONS DELEGATES and other distinguished visitors looked at the low sandy islands of Jaluit Atoll and shook their heads. How, they asked one another, could men gain a livelihood here with the meager resources of this far outpost of civilization? How could the United Nations, far away at Lake Success, Long Island, understand the problems of these island peoples? Could the United States, now Trustee of this, the Trust Territory of the Pacific Islands, administer it wisely? One visitor asked these questions of the lady skipper of the *Morning Star*.

"Miss Wilson, you have been out here for a long time, I understand. In your opinion, can the United States do the right kind of job here in these islands without great expense, which Congress might not underwrite?"

Eleanor smiled. "In my opinion, yes," she said, realizing something of the dilemma of a stranger attempting to understand life in these island chains in a brief visit. "You know that these island peoples have maintained themselves here for centuries, for fifteen hundred years, if we can believe the anthropologists. They do not want or require a standard of living such as ours. What we must do is to market their copra for them. It is their only money crop, besides a very small income derived from the sale of the Trochus shell, which Japan buys for its button factories. They must receive some food and most of their clothing from outside. But most of all, they need encouragement—the sure knowledge that they are not forgotten by the world but have a rightful place in it. Remember, they have survived the raids of Spanish pirates and slavers and the domination of both Germans and Japanese. They have been thrust abruptly from their simple culture pattern into our complex modern one and their adjustment to it has been extraordinary. They endured the frightful bombings in the last war—a war in which they had no stake. They have had the atolls of Bikini and Eniwetok taken from them to be used as a testing ground for our nuclear weapons. These dispossessed people have had to start life anew on other islands. And they do not hate us! I think that speaks well for their Christian spirit."

The visitor was listening with profound attention. Plainly he wished to learn all he could from the experience of the lady missionary.

"Do you know what Admiral Wright said after his tour of Micronesia?" Eleanor asked. The visitor shook his head. "I will try to quote him exactly. 'If the western world were wiped out, there might go forth from these islands a purer kind of Christianity than the world has known before.'"

Eleanor did not try to amplify this statement. Her listener was plainly more than a little startled at its significance.

Missionaries! Until now he had never thought too highly of them. They were conscientious and well-meaning, of course, but often they tried to impose unsuitable standards on people who would have been much happier left alone! But, he understood now, the world had not left the islanders alone and that it had remained in large part for the missionaries to help them adjust to the modern world. Their old pagan beliefs would inevitably have perished on contact with a more complex civilization. What would have replaced them if the Christian missionaries had not come? The visitor came to understand swiftly that the spiritual needs of the islanders were as urgent as their temporal ones, perhaps even more so. This idea was a little more than he had bargained for.

"I see," he said slowly. "The island people here have been between the upper and nether millstone. The United

States has a unique opportunity to do a fine thing here—before the eyes of the whole world."

He hesitated a moment, then said, "We hear that the Soviet Union wants some Marshallese people sent to the United Nations to testify publicly whether or not they are being mistreated under the trusteeship of the United States."

Eleanor smiled. "You need have no fear. I think our government is doing all it can and is improving its methods as it learns by experience, which is the only way any organization, public or private, can learn. No one, European or Asiatic, can understand the psychology of the Marshallese or Caroline Island peoples overnight. They have a perception in judging people that is, I believe, superior to ours. They do not need to know the alien language to tell correctly if a person is good or bad. I have found their judgment of strangers to be invariably right. I believe any anthropologist will bear me out."

"So," the visitor said. He made careful notes of the facts he wished to remember. Then turning to Eleanor with new respect, he asked, "Exactly when did your missionaries arrive here?"

"We came to Kusaie and Ponape in the Carolines back in 1852. In just two years we shall celebrate our one-hundredth anniversary there. We reached the Marshall Islands in 1857 when we had our first mission ship. The remoter islands were converted by Marshallese Christians, so that on some islands our churches are only fifty years old."

Neither noticed the "we" instead of "they" for the missionaries of yesteryear. They were one in spirit with the speaker and this the stranger well understood.

"Nearly a century in these islands!" The visitor's voice had a Continental inflection. "One can only admire the fortitude of those earnest people. Even today these islands are remote. In that time they must have seemed as far from home as the mountains on the moon."

"And your sailing ship . . ." he went on. "I saw the name, a most poetic name, too—*Morning Star VI*. I take it there have been five others since, was it 1857?"

Eleanor nodded.

"Some philanthropist in your rich country gave these ships, I presume?" He was sure of an affirmative answer. Since church and state were separate in the United States, they could not have been purchased with public funds.

"Not at all," Eleanor answered. "These ships were bought for the most part by the Sunday School children of our churches from New England to Hawaii in purchases of shares in the ship at ten cents each!"

"Fabulous!" The gentleman stared at his informant. She was, he had been told, a minister of the gospel of a sect called Congregationalist, a word which to him conveyed relatively little. A nonconformist sect, no doubt like the Pilgrims and the Puritans who had settled on Plymouth Rock. This would be a matter of history in which certainly she would not mislead him. Yet in his rather wide governmental and journalistic experience, he had learned that there were no absolutes. Yet this appeared to be just that— an unbelievable truth.

"Your work was financed like that, from the small donations of children, and it prospered?" His voice showed his astonishment.

"We planted the seed," Eleanor answered quietly. "The Lord gave the increase."

He looked fixedly at the lady missionary, as if trying to penetrate behind her words.

"It would appear that He did," he said. "One judges by the evidence. The young men in positions of authority now in the islands—they are for the most part graduates of your school and, I understand, the sons or grandsons of pastors and missionaries. It is a notable record, madam! Permit me to congratulate you on a very great achievement. I am glad that I have had this opportunity of talking with you. It is a privilege."

He bowed with European grace. He was not dressed in morning coat or striped trousers, but something of the diplomat remained. His light-weight suit was a sad mass of wrinkles. It was the best he had been able to purchase, and it was still too warm for this equatorial climate. On the plane he resolved to remove his collar and tie. To do so here, speaking to a lady of clerical calling, was to him unthinkable.

"I wish I could visit some of your missions," he said. "How many of them are there?"

"In the Marshalls, we have a Mission on each of the twenty-three inhabited atolls. You know there are a few barren atolls where no one lives; the people visit them only to harvest the coconuts. We have a mission on Mejij and on Elip—single islands which are just dots in the sea and are not on an atoll at all. Then we have an elementary boarding school on Rong Rong in Majuro Atoll."

"And your church pays for all this?"

"Not any more. The Association of Marshall Island Churches is now financially independent of the American Mission Board. I am here only as a helper and advisor."

"Most interesting and, I may add, enlightening. What the church has done, surely an organized state or collection of states should be able to do. . . ." He hesitated, then added graciously, "If they approach the problem with the same spirit of devotion and desire to be of service. May I wish you well, madam, in your work? To know you, even for this little, has been a privilege!"

The day after the *Star's* arrival at Imroij, the Dri Komit, or Church Committe, of the atoll convened. Eleanor watched with real pleasure the efficient manner in which they conducted all business. She had brought lumber and roofing to build a temporary shelter house on Jabwor for the use of anyone who went back to plant his land. She had food aboard the *Star* for a work party. Immediately twenty-five able-bodied men volunteered to do the work. Money was not even mentioned. This was a community project and everyone was glad to help. From earliest days the building of a house or a canoe had been a happy occasion to which the most skilled were proud to contribute. Eleanor thought of the roof raisings and husking bees of colonial America.

Where Jabwor Mission had stood was now only ruin. The wooden church, the native-built houses for teachers and students of the school, had been flattened. Incendiary bombs had set fires that had gutted the ruins. The Japanese had been using the mission buildings, and they had been a natural target. Only the reinforced cement kitchen remained standing, and it was open to the winds where it had once joined the wooden mission house. The land on all sides was pockmarked with bomb craters.

Eleanor thought of the Reverend Carl Heine, the Australian missionary, whom she had visited here shortly before the war. How sad it was that he had not lived to see peace come to his islands and with it the hope that he might visit America—a land he had never seen and yet dearly loved. Indeed, he had once asked Eleanor if she guessed why he wore a goatee.

"No," she answered, "but it becomes you."

He laughed with pleasure. "I wear it because I want to look like Uncle Sam!"

He had paid with his life for his love of all things American. He had been beheaded by the Japanese in 1944 on suspicion of American sympathies. For years they had not permitted him to leave the islands for fear he might betray some information about their fortification. His son and daughter-in-law had vanished at the time of his execution. They were last seen running for a canoe to escape from Imig. They were never heard from again.

Yet Carl Heine's influence had not been destroyed. On other islands his children and grandchildren escaped. His son, Bourn, was principal of the school at Rong Rong; his daughter, Josephine, a pastor's wife, worked with her husband on Likiep; his grandson, Dwight Heine, had been a Navy interpreter and was now at the University of Hawaii; his granddaughter, Mary, had served as interpreter for a famous anthropologist working in the Marshalls. She was married to Isaac Lanwi, a young hospital corpsman who had been sent to Guam for medical training. It was no surprise to Eleanor when some time later young "Dr. Isaac" became the famous oculist of the Trust Territory and Dwight, Superintendent of Schools of the Marshall Islands. Isaac, Dwight and Mary had all been students at the mission school in Kusaie before the war.

Eleanor stayed only two days at Jabwor. Before she left, the framework of the shelter house was up. The roof was on and the floor had been laid. The women would make pandanus thatch for the walls. Soon this bombed out island, now overgrown with lush tropical vines, would be cleared and replanted with coconut, breadfruit, and bananas. In three to five years, people could return here to live. The workers of the land, called the Dri Jerabal, now lived on a neighboring island where the people freely shared their food with them. The Iroij, or feudal noble who owned the land, often lived elsewhere, returning periodically to look after land and people and to collect the copra for sale. No one needed to stay here to plow or harrow. Nature was prodigal in this equatorial climate wherever there was sufficient soil. Only now and then need workers come to cut back the vines that would choke the young trees.

Fortunately there were tools, many of them provided by the U. S. Navy while the people were refugees on Majuro. When Kwajalein and Majuro had been taken by the Americans, United States Navy ships lay off these atolls to evacuate the Marshallese from Islands still held by Japan. A Marshallese was sent ashore to tell the people they might now escape to Majuro, which had not been bombed and where there was food. And so by night the hungry people had stolen out in perilously overladen outrigger canoes to have their first full meal since the war began. Some brought a few pigs and chickens that the Japanese rulers had not yet eaten. All knew that on unbombed Majuro their brother islanders would gladly share with them whatever they had. America's responsibility had begun.

CHAPTER IX

All Over Micronesia

THE *Star* STARTED BACK to Kwajalein, its hold empty, but she had passengers—workers who had been delegated to secure roofing for the new church they were building at Imroij. Their journey northwest up the chain of islands was broken by stops at Ailinglaplap and at Namu on church business. At Namu there was a dispute over the land on which the church and pastor's house stood. It was a considerable stretch of land for Namu, equal perhaps to half a city block.

Land in the Marshall Islands is held on a strictly feudal basis closely resembling the pattern of medieval Europe. Society is composed of three classes: noble, half-noble and commoner. It is perhaps closer to the ancient Scottish clan system where the chief exacted absolute obedience from, and accepted absolute responsibility for, the welfare of every clansman. Each class had certain definite rights to its share of the produce of the land, even the humblest commoner or Dri Jerabal (worker), who had no hope of becoming a landowner. He worked the land on shares, giving a percentage to the Iroij who owned the land and another to the Alap, or head of his maternal clan. This percentage usually was not exorbitant. It varied, but in general it amounted to four per cent for the noble and six per cent for the family head. No island child was born without the right to honorable subsistence. There were no paupers; and since in the

Marshalls and in other areas of Micronesia inheritance is entirely through the mother's clan, illegitimacy is no bar to inheritance.

Eleanor thought she understood the matrilinear succession but she kept encountering problems in both ownership of land and the use of its products which baffled her. Even after many years in the islands, she felt lost in the maze of native custom. One day she consulted the anthropologist at Majuro, who had made a special study of this problem. Mr. Jack Tobin shook his head.

"I don't wonder you are puzzled. I've been working on it as a full-time job and I'm still running into new ramifications. Basically, the land is divided into three categories. The Bwij or maternal lineage land is only one of these, though it is the most common and the most important."

"I understand," Eleanor said, "that when the eldest female dies, both the leadership of the lineage and responsibility over the land go to her brother or sister, next in age. When all of these brothers and sisters are dead, the maternal lands go to the eldest child of the eldest female child and so on down. Is this right?"

"Yes. But if that child is a woman or a man advanced in age, and physically or mentally incompetent, then a younger and abler person normally looks after the land for the head of the family. For example, Judge Kabua, who is the chief or Iroij, looks after his family land for his elder sister.

Then he added, "However, it isn't that simple! All land is not Bwij or family land. There is another type of land tenure called Ninnin land. It means literally 'nurse from the breast,' and is land allocated by a parent to his own child. By some curious ancient custom, this can be done in certain instances. Disputes arise when some islander claims this privilege and the head of the family does not agree."

"Oh, dear, I can see lots of ground for dispute," Eleanor ejaculated. "I remember what a time they had on Arno when two nobles made rival claims to the same land."

Tobin nodded. He had been involved in that case.

"It is very much like conditions in medieval Europe. It is very interesting to see the parallel between various civilizations. In this nonindustrial society, land is the only basis of value and these disputes seem inevitable. And besides the Bwij lands and the Ninnin lands, there is a third class, the Divided lands. In the old days these were given by the Iroij for special service in war or peace. For a long time it was the custom for the Iroij to give land to those who nursed him in his old age. We now have the additional problem of returning the land taken by various governments over the past fifty years. After all these years, the problem of who has prior claim can be a knotty one."

"We will give it back to the descendants of the Iroij or chief from whom it was taken?" Eleanor asked quickly.

Tobin replied, "It is planned to return it to *all* of the people whose forebears possessed rights in the land, according to the recognized Marshallese custom. This would include both chiefs and commoners. The question of returning it directly to the commoners has now come up. That is thought to be more consistent with our democratic system. But many people think we are asking for trouble if we upset the ancient land inheritance pattern of the islands. But change is coming. In fact, it has commenced even here. I think both nobles and commoners feel it. Naturally, the former wish to retain their rights and the latter wish to gain new rights in keeping with the times."

Eleanor nodded. "Isn't gradual change the best way, rather than to make new and startling rules?"

"Yes," Tobin agreed. "People do not like to have their pattern of culture blasted from under them. I am sure we would react in the same way."

"I suppose one of the principal services an anthropologist can render is to study thoroughly the customs of the people —so he may advise both the government and the people and minimize friction between them."

"That's exactly right from my point of view," Tobin

agreed. "The research done here should be directed to that end."

The church's land problem on Namu involved the Alap and his relatives, not all of whom were church members. This church, therefore, was in the odd position of using the land and, like a worker, owing to the Alap of a family and its Iroij the customary share of the produce of this land. Rarely, if ever, was this share asked for or expected, but after the war the question was raised by a relative of the Alap regarding the right of the church to the use of the land. The matter was referred to the Association of Marshall Island Churches, in whose behalf Eleanor consulted the Alap. It was for this she had stopped at Namu.

The Alap, who administered these lands for his mother's family, assured her he was quite satisfied to have the church there. As in many other legal disputes, the dissatisfied relative was nowhere to be found.

At Namu, Eleanor was faced with the age-old problem of every ship captain who touched these islands—a plethora of would-be passengers. One American captain of a large vessel called his ship the *Stowaway Special,* for it was impossible to tell his crew from his deck passengers and these from the stowaways. One Namu Island woman requested passage and was granted it, but when she arrived she was accompanied by three adults and two children. They brought some food and drinking nuts, but, if the *Star* had been becalmed, there would have been six extra mouths to feed, and the question of water would have been critical. But this troubled only the lady skipper. The islanders took literally the biblical injunction to take no thought for the morrow. Indeed, they took none for it long before the Bible was translated into island tongues.

The *Star* left Namu at noon, and by dark, the lights of Kwajalein made a glow in the sky and the flash of the port beacon marked off the seconds. Even had the compass failed them, they would still have made Kwajalein that night.

It was May 9th when Eleanor reported to the Port Director, not without some inward satisfaction; for contrary to all supposition, the *Star* had made a successful voyage—a voyage in the true sense of a return to its home port. The Port Director had news for her, too.

"Miss Wilson," he said with real pleasure, "your ship is coming in!"

"*My* ship! You mean the *Rochester?*" Eleanor exclaimed.

"Yes. And from the look on your face, I suspect you have a sweetheart aboard her!"

Eleanor laughed. "I have. My nephew, Dr. Theodore Wilson. Do you suppose I might go out with the pilot to meet him?"

"I'm afraid I can't allow that, but I can send you out with the mail. I presume they'll anchor not far from the Pass."

But rumor carried the word on the pilot boat that Miss Eleanor Wilson was coming, and when she stepped from the mail boat to the landing platform of the ship's stair she was greeted by a bear hug from a young naval officer. A thousand necks were craned to see who the young ship's doctor was hugging, and with the Captain looking on and not saying a word! Certainly no other young Navy officer was welcomed to Kwajalein by a kiss from his maiden aunt. Had the ship put in a few days later, she would have been gone. This meeting, to Eleanor, was the biggest single thrill in her long years of foreign service. She could not go home for months to come, but on a United States Navy ship, home had come to her.

On May 24th she received a radiogram from Boston with orders to proceed to Truk to attend a meeting of Micronesian missionaries. This meant that for the time being she must desert her ship and turn her attention to the general work of the missions. The *Star* was safe in Kwajalein Atoll and Commander Whitney, a Navy medical man stationed at the base, promised to keep a watchful eye on her.

Luckily transportation was available. A Navy ship, an AKL, was leaving Kwajalein within three days for the Carolines. Eleanor reached Truk in the record time of six days, only to find that she was one day too late! The meetings had ended the day before. She had come nine hundred miles for nothing. And as for returning, there was no direct transportation for her from Truk to the Marshalls. The only other route was by way of Guam in the Marianas, a detour of some thirteen hundred miles. No plane seat was available even by this roundabout way for a month to come. This was one of the frustrations of travel in the Trust Territory.

She used the month to preach, with Anna Dederer, a German missionary at Truk, for her interpreter; to prepare teaching helps for the Sunday School lessons in Marshallese; and to write a six months' report for the folks back home in Boston. She spoke at the summer session of PITTS (Pacific Island Teachers' Training School) attended by students from all over the Trust Territory. Here she spoke in English, for the Caroline Islands have no common language. Either they were peopled by settlers of widely different stock, or, being so isolated over the centuries, developed divergent tongues. On Kapingamarangi, a tiny dot on the equator south of Ponape, the people, being of pure Polynesian stock, spoke a true Polynesian dialect. Only in the Marshalls could the people understand one another freely.

Eleanor looked about her at the faces of the young Micronesian people who would soon be teachers in the schools of the Trust Territory.

"I wish our first missionaries who came to these islands could see all of you here at this fine school. I am sure they would feel richly rewarded for the labor, the trials, and the dangers they encountered. It is hard to remember now, how isolated these islands once were. When the chartered ship, and later the *Morning Stars,* sailed away, the people had no communication with the outside world. Once, back in the Spanish days, our missionaries were saved by the timely arrival of an American ship.

"Remember that the great work of those missionaries was translating the Bible into many languages. The work is far from complete but most of you have at least the gospels and the psalms in your own language.

"I want to compliment you on the wonderful progress you have made in your work. I think it is remarkable that you learn to read and study so quickly in an entirely new tongue. Perhaps no other Territory has so many languages. It is hard to explain to people back home in the States that a Pelauan cannot speak to a person from Yap or Truk; that Ponapean is understood only in Ponape and the adjacent islands of Mokil and Pingelap; that even in the Marshalls, where there is only one basic language, there are many different words in the Ralik and the Radak chains, and even a ceremonial language different from both of these.

"Then, too, so many of you as children learned Japanese; some of the older people, German; and a few still older, Spanish. And now nearly all of your speak some English and you are improving every day."

Pleased looks passed over the faces of the students at PITTS. They did have many difficulties to overcome, not only of language but of custom, and to grow used to the restraint of school and study, so different from the outdoor life they knew. It was good to be praised! It stimulated them to greater effort.

"You are going out to be teachers in your home islands or islands nearby. You must not be downcast if you encounter difficulties. Just think of the wonderful progress made in Micronesia in just a hundred years—a very short time after all. You may not have enough books, at least not as many as you would like. But these will come. Remember, the first teachers and missionaries had fewer still. You have your Bibles and basic schoolbooks. You must learn to make do."

Eleanor paused, letting this point drive home.

"Back in America, we have a definition of the Ideal University. It is a professor sitting on one end of a log and a student on the other! Many of our great men had very little schooling. Abraham Lincoln had only a few terms in a country school. He had the will to learn and he walked many miles after his day's work to borrow a book from a neighbor. I am sure you are all willing to do the same."

There were nods of understanding and approval. They clapped vigorously. They knew they would have little to work with on many a distant atoll. Well, if others had done this, so could they. There was no ennui at PITTS. Study was a privilege. All were glad to be there. To Eleanor it was an inspiring sight to see so many young Micronesians going out to teach their own people. She wished the first missionaries could see this school. How many dark days they must have lived through, when it seemed their efforts were in vain and that they could make no impression on the dark superstitions that bound the islanders.

While on Moen Island, where the school was located, Eleanor met Chief Petrus of Truk, whom she regarded as a kind of Abraham Lincoln of this island group. His quiet wisdom, his great dignity, his ability to think clearly and to express himself with courtesy, even when his opinions were in direct opposition to those about him, singled him out as a natural leader. A judge without a bench, his integrity was well known and his decisions were rarely questioned. When there were no records of who owned a piece of land, he was consulted. If he said it belonged to this or that branch of a certain family, they might claim it unchallenged. Only the boundary lines were often curiously twisted, that is, from the point of view of an outsider, such as an American Land Claims Officer. In one instance, these lines completely encircled a single breadfruit tree whose rich yield no Moen Islander would claim. It had been planted expressly for a certain honored guest who came often to visit a local family. They did not want her to feel that she was dependent on them for food, so they gave her her own tree and its yield was hers. It was an act of true courtesy that Eleanor could appreciate.

It was June 28th when she caught the Navy plane for Guam, twenty-one hundred miles home by a roundabout route, northwest to the Marianas and then back southeast to the Marshalls—a dog's leg of a journey if there ever was one. But she showed no annoyance. The Navy had always been most cooperative, and she would not complain because this once they could not conveniently fly her directly back to Kwajalein. She wondered in what condition she would find the *Star!* Would the decks be scrubbed, the brass shined, the bedding aired, and the men's cabins in a decent state of cleanliness? From past experience, she had her doubts. She shrugged. She had become half-islander at heart. "Take no thought for the morrow." Her father had always said that meant, "Take no undue thought for the morrow." Well, no one could quarrel with the last phrase of the quotation. "Sufficient unto the day is the evil thereof."

CHAPTER X

Back to Rong Rong Mission

"NEW SAILS!" Eleanor almost shouted in her excitement at seeing the brand-new canvas bending on the *Star*. "And the engine's fixed!"

There was no mistaking those fresh white sails nor the puffs of smoke coming out of the exhaust pipe at the stern. This was almost too good to be true, after so many heartbreaking disappointments. Tears filled her eyes. With auxiliary power and new sails, they could now go among reefs and islands with confidence. Under sail alone it was a precarious business. She knew it was mainly good luck and fair winds that had brought them back safely from their shakedown cruise to Jaluit Atoll. But now they would set out properly equipped. Well, the jinx was broken!

Clement, the engineer, was beaming. The engine went chug-chug with more assurance than at any time he could remember. What made it do so had never been entirely clear to him, though he had read the manual diligently. At least half the words had been incomprehensible to him, but he was used to that. It was so when he read his Bible. Only the wise could be expected to understand the printed word altogether.

The Fourth of July was a holiday, and the commanding officer at the Boat Pool said he and his men would take a trial spin on the *Star* to make sure the engine was all right. The excitement of all hands aboard was understandable. They sailed out of Bigej Pass, around the Kwajalein end of the Atoll and in at South Pass. The wind was fresh, the sun beneficent, and everyone relaxed for the day. The Navy men pronounced themselves quite satisfied with the engine's performance.

Four days later the *Star* set sail for Majuro, but after chugging along for about twenty-five miles, the engine stopped dead. It was much easier to sail west than east with the prevailing winds, so they returned, quite dispirited, to Kwajalein.

The Boat Pool men groaned audibly as they saw the *Star*, but they tried again and finally got the engine working. Plainly, poor Clement could not have passed the Navy rating for engineer!

On July 11th, the *Star* again turned its bow toward the home port of Majuro. They were hardly out of the pass when the engine coughed and spat, like a balky automobile engine starting reluctantly and dying again on a nippy winter morning in a cold garage. Another cough and it stopped altogether. The *Star* could not hold her course with this loss of power. Her momentum carried her forward for a few lengths, then she veered and her sails spilled their wind. A kind of cry went up from the men's throats, not so much a wail as an exhalation of anguish.

"Not so soon!" Eleanor exclaimed. "Oh, surely the engine can't break down so soon!" She rushed down the ladder. Clement, his hands covered with grease, was standing helplessly over the dead motor.

"Can't you do *something*, Clement!" she exclaimed.

He shook his head sadly. "Mother Wilson, I'll try. I worked only on Japanese boats, but Japanese motors were all different."

How she wished that a course in mechanics had been included in the curriculum of the theological seminary!

Her heart sank. They were right back in the nineteenth century! It was one thing to keep the *Star* on the right course when one went straight toward one's objective, and quite another to do so when they were crisscrossing that course many times a day at the sport of the wind. But she knew there was no other way. A ship can sail with a following wind, or with the wind on her quarter, but if she must sail into the wind as they were now, it could be done only by a long series of tacks. Of this she knew nothing and must, therefore, leave the sailing entirely to Anliri. She would have to be doubly diligent in keeping some sort of track of their course by dead reckoning and seize every opportunity to get star sights to fix their position.

Due to adverse winds they found themselves off Ailing-laplap southeast of Kwajalein on July 12th and off Maloelap, northeast of their starting point, on the 14th. From Maloe-lap the winds were favorable, and on the next day they sighted Majuro.

"Good!" Eleanor said, beaming proudly at her crew. "We shall sleep ashore tonight."

Anliri shook his head. "Then you must pray, Mother Wilson! All by myself, I do not think I can take the *Star* through the pass. We have not enough wind and the current is against us!"

Then he called something in Marshallese that she could not catch, and the crew to a man sprang to reef sail. There was the ugly green water that marked the reef! Oh, if only they had the engine now! What skill could keep the *Star* off that reef? Would they have to turn and head out to sea again under these lowering skies? If only a Navy boat would come along and tow them in! But they might not have been sighted from the Coast Guard Station on Rong Rong, and they were more than half the lagoon's length from the base at Uliga, so there was small hope of aid.

It was this night that she learned how fully she could trust her island-born crew. They might not keep the ship as clean as a visiting admiral could wish; they might be stubborn about not following a compass course; but, by all that was good and true, they could sail!

They were in their element—on a ship with only wind for power, fighting green shoal water and the jagged coral reef.

Anliri called an order, and it was instantly obeyed. Back and forth they tacked all night long, fighting the current which threatened momentarily to drag them on the reef. Eleanor prayed for strength to face with calmness whatever the night might bring. There was never a show of fear, never a sign of panic on the part of her crew. They went about their accustomed business, unconcerned.

Then the first streak of light began to show in the east. A cry went up from Freddy, on watch at the prow. One sweeping gesture of the sailing master's arm, the helm spun, and the *Star* caught the now incoming tide, and swept through the pass and into the more sheltered, if still dangerous, waters of Majuro Lagoon. The men shouted, not in relief, but with the joy of children. Yet even now they could not relax, for all the way to Rong Rong the lagoon was dotted with coral heads—isolated pieces of hard coral thrusting up from the bottom, that could tear a gaping hole in the hull of the *Star*.

Eleanor marveled at these men. They seemed to show no ill effects of a night of labor or terror. She was exhausted, worn out by the sleepless, anxious night. They proceeded cautiously to their anchorage off Rong Rong.

She had been gone from home more than two months, and it was high time she was getting back. Odd how one set of worries quite blotted out another! Wasn't it Lloyd George who once said that a change of worries was as good as a rest? Well, she did not agree with him, for she could not feel that she had had any rest during her absence. Yet while worrying about the *Star* and about the work on Truk, all cares of her customary tasks at Rong Rong had been left behind. Now she must pick up the threads again.

Was her tiny "home" still standing? Had the ants gotten into her stock of staple food? Had the cockroaches, with a passion for learning, eaten portions of her books?

When the anchors were thrown out and the *Star* was headed into the wind, off their own mission shore, she said quietly, "Now we will hold morning prayers."

Every head was bowed. It was the routine of the ship, but this morning they were especially fervent. It had been hard to spend a night in danger so close to home and safety. It was mid-morning when all was secured aboard the *Star* and they could go ashore.

As the dinghy bore the seafarers ashore, students, teachers, and neighbors rushed to the water's edge to grasp the hands of the lady skipper and her island crew. There was always a great deal of handshaking in the islands. Eleanor was "home."

Her house at Rong Rong was still standing. Eleanor, with a heart full of joy and satisfaction, climbed the five steep wooden steps to her castle on the sand. She opened the door. How nice it looked! There on her desk was her Bible just as she had left it. No, not *just* as she had left it, for the cockroaches had eaten the edges off the *Pentateuch,* and some creature, probably a silverfish moth, had gutted a neat circular line deep down through all the pages to *Revelation!* Well, she could still use it for study purposes, and she had another Bible aboard ship. The house would have to be scrubbed and sprayed before she could think of spending a night in it. Something eternally feminine in Eleanor Wilson struggled to make a neat and orderly home even of a few boards on a strip of coral sand. Where New Englanders go, they take New England with them. But not beyond Hawaii could their architecture assert itself! Here on the low atolls one lived in houses much like the thatched huts of the islanders.

Something brushed against her leg. Instinctively Eleanor recoiled. Then she looked down and laughed. It was Rascal, her cat, daughter of Henrietta, ship's cat of the *Star,* who had signed on at Panama! Rascal, with true missionary zeal, despised a bad name and refused to answer to that sobriquet! Unless one called, "Kitty, kitty, kitty," she went in the opposite direction. It was not hard to guess where Henrietta had found a mate, for she had been allowed to go ashore on Kusaie. Cats have a pride of their own which is above

and beyond all genealogy. Certainly Rascal, or Kitty, did not
care. She looked hopefully at her mistress with an air of
waiting eagerly, albeit with dignity, that did not escape
Eleanor.

"Yes, Rascal, you shall have some fish right quick."

She picked her up and stroked her gray and white fur.
She was one warm little living thing in the desolation of
her insect-invaded house. If Eleanor had to open the last
prized can of salmon, Kitty should have her fish!

The girl students could and would clean her house. She
had more pressing business than scrubbing, with all the mission and school affairs to be put in order. She had left Rong
Rong Mission in the care of Bourn Heine, the local principal. He was a good and conscientious man and would have
done his best, she knew. He had some of the rare gifts of his
famous father, the Reverend Carl Heine, who would always
be a legend among the islands. He had made service to his
adopted islands his life work. Not in every generation did
the genius in a family come out. In Bible days, Isaac had
been the link between two men of dominant personality, his
father, Abraham, and his son, Jacob. So with Bourn.

He was standing by the "library" when she went out to
call some girls to help her. Andrew Carnegie would have
snorted at the name "library," for this was but a one-room,
board shack. Still, they had been glad enough to have it in
1946 when every piece of lumber that could be salvaged
from old Navy installations was precious. The library had
quite a past! It had once stood on Laura, church headquarters of Majuro Atoll, and had been floated on old empty
kerosene drums out onto the lagoon and then towed at low
tide by the men of the church to Rong Rong. One end of
the library had been her bedroom when she lived on Laura.
Bourn was able to make good use of the books because he
knew English well. It was a great advantage to him as school
principal to speak almost equally well the language of his
students and the language in which their books were
printed. There were so few books in Marshallese—only parts

of the Bible, the hymnal, *Pilgrim's Progress,* and an arithmetic.

When Bourn smiled, his gold-crowned tooth shone in the sunlight. Most islanders have poor teeth and need dentures by middle life. Eleanor recalled that this characteristic had been passed on to the descendants of the *Bounty's* mutineers by their Polynesian mothers. Was it lack of meat in the island diet even today or the predilection for the sweets the foreigners had introduced? It certainly added to the problems of the government, for dentistry in the islands until the Navy came had been crude. She recalled with compassion the troubles of poor Miss Jane Baldwin, the veteran missionary of Kusaie, in securing a set of "store teeth" back in Japanese days. These had been an indifferent success. Eleanor herself had made the impressions with a kind of plaster of Paris, supplied by the Japanese dentist on Ponape, three hundred miles away. She had mixed the powder as directed until it formed a gelatinous mass. This had been molded around Miss Baldwin's toothless gums, and she had sat like a martyr until it hardened. These impressions had been sent to Ponape and in due course, months later, the dentures arrived. Lucky the missionary in these islands who needed neither dentures nor eyeglasses.

One island pastor wore his precious dentures—carefully fitted in Japan—only to church; the moment the meeting was over he took them out and put them in his coat pocket. Once, however, when his wife laundered his white coat, she did not notice them in the pocket. Whang went the laundry paddle, and the dentures were reduced to fragments. The pastor had a clean suit, but never again did he have any new dentures.

Many things were pressing for Eleanor's attention. Bourn was smiling at her.

"It is so good to have you back, Mother Wilson," he said thankfully. "There is so much I must ask you. So many problems I cannot settle alone!" His heart was here on Rong Rong, and they needed Mother Wilson so badly. It was hard to spare her even to the *Star.*

Once more she fell into the routine of the mission school, but somehow it did not absorb her whole attention. Part of her remained aboard the *Star,* tossing at its anchorage offshore. Had she gotten some salt water in her blood or, like the Marshallese themselves, become something of a sea gypsy, longing to sail on any ship anywhere—just for a change? This was not hard to understand. Life could be monotonous on a low atoll where there was nowhere to go except to another stretch of sand where one might sit under a nearly identical coconut tree! No wonder young American seamen, newly out from the States, went "rock happy." Yes, she was getting rock happy, and, therefore, she welcomed the chance to go over to the main island of Majuro.

The largest island of each atoll took its name from that of the atoll as a whole. So at Kwajalein, Kwajalein Island was the largest dot on its reef.

Majuro Island was situated at the southwest side of the atoll. Uliga, the Navy headquarters, was far to the eastern end of the chain. Majuro was quite a place—at least by island standards. Its people boasted they could walk all of eight miles in one direction without getting their feet wet. And by wetting one's feet, one could go over the little chain of islands to Uliga. The tiniest dot of an island on the reef, even if it bore only one coconut tree, had an owner. In this world of sea, every handful of soil that could grow food was precious. Virtually no land was ever sold, for what was there in island economy of equal value? Land grew food, and food was life. A person who owned many coconut palms and breadfruit trees was rich. Indeed, only the Iroij or nobles might own land. Yet workers never went hungry. They were by well established custom allowed a share that provided them with an adequate living. If they were sick, the Iroij (a kind of feudal overlord) paid their hospital expenses. If they were lazy, their relatives supported them. There were no beggars in the island, nor was their need to legislate "social security." They had it as part of their birthright.

The succession of land—through the maternal side—had

its curious consequences, particularly when it became en-
tangled with island tabus. There was one man on a certain
atoll famous for his unusual misfortune. He alone of all the
Marshallese belonged to no family, had no relatives, no right
to any share of the produce of the land. He lived entirely
upon the charity of his adopted mother. When she died, it
was questionable whether her relatives would recognize
his claim to her land.

His case was unique. Born a twin, his twin was a girl. The
islanders had been horrified. One of their sex tabus had
been violated—a brother had touched his sister in the mother's womb. The boy was instantly buried in a hastily made
shallow grave to hide the family's shame. A neighbor, being
childless and pitying the baby, dug it up and reared it as her
own. But in island society the boy was a nameless outcast
without clan or family connections. He grew to manhood
having no part in island society.

Fortunately for him his twin sister learned from Christian
teachers that her brother had committed no crime, that his
birth was normal and that the family had no cause to feel
shame. She insisted that he be acknowledged a son and be
given his full rights of inheritance. To him this came as a
direct miracle, and his gratitude to his compassionate sister was beyond telling.

There were people who said we should not send missionaries, that the islanders were happier in their pagan beliefs!
How well Eleanor knew that "happiness"! Even her parishioners, all staunch adherents of the Christian Church, were
loath to sleep in a room without a light, for fear of ghosts.
The wartime blackout enforced by the Japanese had been a
particular hardship to them. Belief in and fear of evil
spirits was not yet dead. Light might not scare a ghost away,
but at least one could see it and be forewarned.

Eleanor left Rong Rong for Majuro Island one bright
July morning. There was no need to take the *Star* for so
short a journey. Instead, they took the *Little Star,* an eight-

een-foot sailboat that Eleanor would have liked to call the *Starlet*. She looked forward to her visit to the "metropolis," for Majuro Island had eight hundred inhabitants and even a town called Laura, in Navy code. It had small stores, a dispensary, a public school, a Quonset hut that housed the offices of the island magistrate and his scribe, and the council meeting hall. Many tall coconut palms grew on its beaches and there were large cultivated patches of taro. Better still, papaya trees flourished. The papaya fruit, somewhat resembling a melon, is the true island delicacy. Comparatively, life on Majuro was luxurious. Dr. Alexander Spoehr of Bishop Museum, Honolulu, had chosen it for his research in anthropology. One of her mission students, Mary Heine Lanwi, had been his interpreter.

The *Little Star* went safely through the jagged rocky pass into the inner lagoon. The anchor was thrown out and a small outrigger canoe shot out from shore to ferry them to the beach. There were shouts of laughter and cries of welcome. In the canoe were some girls from the mission school. A large group of people was waiting on the beach, so it was another homecoming for Eleanor. King Langlan greeted her as if she were his next of kin. Indeed, on her return to the Marshalls after the war, she had lived in his house, dividing her time between Laura and the Carolines. So Laura was her first home in the Marshalls, her second at Rong Rong.

She was delighted to see that her house was swept and ready for her. Oh, the luxury of living under one's own roof! She had not always had this here on Laura. Island hospitality was given with love and courtesy hard to match in this world, but quarters were always limited and privacy a thing almost unknown. How luxurious her house looked— its thatched roof in good repair, its two rooms aired and sweet-smelling, its board floor clean and covered with freshly swept and sunned pandanus mats. The house was well built. Luckabudge had been one of the carpenters. She was "home"!

Eleanor had urgent business at Laura. Anliri, her sailing

master, had a sick wife, and wanted to give up his post. The logical choice to replace him was Mejjon, the pastor at Laura. A relative of Luckabudge, he could also teach him to read waves. Luckabudge could already read clouds and, with Freddy's help, was learning to read the sextant. If he only knew wave patterns, he could count himself a full-fledged navigator. By island custom, Mejjon might be unwilling to part with his knowledge except to a member of his maternal clan.

The first person to appear at her door was the man she most wanted to see—Mejjon himself. He had a large tin tray, much battered and worn, filled with fresh drinking nuts. They refreshed themselves before getting down to business.

"Mejjon," Eleanor said, "you once captained a mission boat. How would you like to take Anliri's place as sailing master of the *Morning Star?*"

Mejjon's face lighted. "I would like it very much, Mother Wilson, only my first care is the church here. I must find someone to take my place."

Things usually move with maddening slowness under the tropic sun, but for once all was quickly arranged. Caesar, a deacon of the church, was willing to take over so Mejjon could go back with Miss Wilson to Rong Rong the following day. For once, Eleanor regretted the haste. She would have liked to linger a day or two here. It was wrong to love luxury, but here, as at Rong Rong, she had her own private bath house close by her dwelling. In it she could soap herself and get a really good fresh-water bath by pouring water from a pail over her head. On the *Star* this was impossible. Only those who have lived in the tropics can truly appreciate what a comfort this was. Back in the States one bathed to be clean. Here one bathed, it seemed, so one could breathe! Cool skin and a clean, ironed dress and privacy.

Eleanor sat alone on the end of her narrow porch overlooking the water. A sense of deep peace and well-being flooded over her. Time, what was it? Not even the greatest astronomer could define it. Out here it was even more ephemeral than at home. Yesterday, today, and tomorrow . . . how they blended. When she was old and back in Cambridge, she would have time to sort out the memories of the long years, perhaps, in orderly fashion. Now they came to her as a chain of incidents that had happened at each place the *Star* or the *Little Star* touched, or as she met islanders who had played a part in them. Some people seemed to have no memories to fill their moments of precious leisure. Eleanor had many and Laura, on Majuro Island, was filled with them.

CHAPTER XI

Life on Majuro Island

ELEANOR HAD RETURNED to Laura in 1946 because the Navy would not permit her to go alone to Kusaie. Mary Heine had been there to act as her interpreter. Mary was the beautiful and talented girl to whom the genius of her grandfather had descended. The island people are natural linguists and learn readily from one another and from outsiders. This gift always amazed Americans, so few of whom ever master any language but their own. Many Marshallese had gone to school in Kusaie and knew Kusaien. Eleanor decided to master Marshallese, telling herself that it could scarcely be more difficult than Kusaien or Japanese.

Before the war she had visited only one atoll in the Marshalls. Yet students from every atoll in the islands had come to her school on Kusaie. So her coming to Laura was not as a stranger but as a beloved teacher and friend. To the Marshallese she was Mother Wilson in every household. Now she was their ordained minister. She remembered seeing tears in the eyes of the people as Mary interpreted her words to them. She told them how earnestly she had prayed for them when she read in the newspapers of the terrible bombings of Kwajalein and Jaluit; and of how she had pleaded with the Mission Board to send her back the moment the war was over.

Mary told her in return what the people of Laura found in their hearts to say—how grateful they were that their Christian brothers in Boston had sent Miss Wilson to them, and how they would help her with all that they had.

Then they had conducted her to the house of their king. There were two kings here on Majuro Island: Langlan, the greater king, and Jitiam, the lesser king. Langlan was known as the greater, as he controlled a larger portion of the land. The Navy had presented each king with a large medallion which bore an eagle and a shield and the word "King." They wore them with modesty on state occasions. Both were highly regarded by the island people.

Langlan's house, to which Eleanor had been conducted in 1946, was made of boards and contained three rooms, all small, with a porch on three sides. It was raised on cement posts well off the ground, making emergency living quarters underneath. Instead of a picturesque thatched roof, it had an efficient if ugly one of corrugated iron. It had, moreover, eaves troughs for carrying rain water into a cement cistern which served the whole neighborhood. And "the grounds" were "landscaped"! There was a huge and very beautiful breadfruit tree that spread its cool comforting shade over yard and porch, besides providing its fruit in its season. The possession of a breadfruit tree was money in the bank at interest and the next best thing to a deepfreeze.

When Eleanor had described the house to her family in Cambridge, it never occurred to her to say that it was one-story. At this time there was no other kind of house in all the islands. No Marshallese woman ever had housemaid's knee from washing stairs; there were none. The few island-ers who had been to Guam or Honolulu, on their return, told disbelieving audiences of the marvels of many-storied buildings. True, some had seen such structures pictured in American movies at Navy posts, but that was in the United States, a place where anything might be expected, judging from the samples, good and bad, of American culture which they had seen since the first Americans landed.

Eleanor's room at the king's house was the best front room, and in it was an iron Navy cot. She had expected to sleep on a mat on the floor. She was really embarrassed by the great pains the king and his people had taken to make her comfortable. The king even assigned a special bathing room in his house for her use. That would have been a real luxury, but Eleanor could not bring herself to use it. The board floor was new, and she would soon have spoiled it. Besides, there was no drainage, and the water must seep through the boards, literally on the heads of the family living under the house! There was, then, no way of bathing except in the lagoon.

She had no bathing suit, but this was not going to stop her. She would make one. But from what? Finally she settled on a top of adequate proportions and a skirt made by the simple process of ripping out one end of a pillowcase. To this costume no censor of the western world could have taken exception. Still, she waited until night, and putting a black cotton kimono over her bathing costume, she set out for the beach, accompanied as always by three "ladies in waiting" whom the king had assigned to her. It would have been most improper for her to venture out at night alone. There was no moon, and the only light came from the stars. Yet, when they reached the beach and Eleanor dropped off her kimono, there were gasps of astonishment from the three Marshallese women. They promptly turned their backs upon her, as modesty demanded. However, when Eleanor had waded into the sea she saw out of the corner of her eye that they were covertly watching her with fascinated curiosity. This was just one more problem for a lady missionary with the simple desire to preserve her habit of a daily bath, even a Marshallese bath in the salt water of the lagoon.

It was after this that she had sent a frantic SOS to the Mission Board secretary in Boston: "Buy me right away a conservative bathing suit with the longest skirt possible."

The secretary groaned at this assignment. "Where," she asked, "can I find such a thing—even in Boston! They just don't make them any more."

But it would be weeks before this much desired costume could possibly arrive. Meanwhile, how good it was to splash about in the cool comfort of the lagoon in the balmy air of the tropic night. She was glad she had not ruined a good cotton dress to swim in. Her stock of dresses would not last long. Not only did the equatorial sun and the constant soaking in salt spray tell on the light fabrics, but they had to endure the merciless beating from the paddles of over-zealous girls who had been assigned to do her laundry. If her clothes escaped the hazards of a Marshallese washing machine—a hole in the coral sand covered with canvas to keep the precious fresh water from seeping away while the clothes were being beaten on a board—they had to endure "trial by fire" from a Japanese charcoal iron. With every care, at times tiny live coals leaped out to burn their way through the fabric. A new dress, after two washings, had lost its pristine elegance; in four, it was already old. In this climate no garment was ever worn more than one day without laundering. Eleanor sighed. What would it be like to step to a clothespress and find silk dresses fresh from the cleaner; or to live in a climate where nylon dresses, which need no ironing, did not suffocate one? The first hard lesson of the tropics is that one wears cotton from the skin out and preferably only one layer of that. And there are no girdles on the equator. Reluctantly she came out of the water, donned the black kimono, and walked up the path to King Langlan's house. Her entourage followed wordlessly. It was difficult for them to grasp that in other lands there must be other customs.

King Langlan's household was a most interesting one. Somehow Eleanor likened him to David at the end of his career. Langlan was very old, just how old no one really knew. In their last census, the Japanese gave his age in the eighties. He was slightly stooped and his ear lobes had been pierced and stretched into long loops like those of his people in pre-European contact days. After all, he had grown to manhood in the 1870's when many of the old customs of the islands were still in force. He had a young wife and a small daughter, his only child. The whole thing seemed quite biblical to Eleanor. To add to this impression were the family names. The king's nephew was called Isaiah. He was the village magistrate; and another relative, Lazarus, was the scribe—not in the sense of the Scribes and Pharisees, but in the sense that he was a writer, a keeper of the records of the court and the register of births and deaths on the island. The king must have shifted his family about to give Eleanor the front room. He, with his wife and child, now lived in a small back room, while Isaiah and his family had moved out onto the side porch. She had never quite understood the exact nature of the relationship of the people living underneath the house to the king's family.

The worst drawback to life at the king's house was the outhouse, which was small, hot, smelly, and unsanitary. Moreover, it had to serve a rather large number of persons. But the very next day after her arrival the men had built a private one for her, of new lumber, and had made a path to it strewn with gleaming white coral sand.

A little sanitation, like a little learning, can be a very dangerous thing. It seemed to Eleanor that it had been infinitely cleaner and more sanitary, as well as much more modest, in primitive times when the islanders went into the sea on the side of the atoll farthest from their homes. The tides made all clean. The famous South Sea Expedition sent out by the Germans in 1910 had made particular note of both the cleanliness and modesty of the islanders in such matters. Indeed, the very mention of such things was tabu, which made it difficult for white doctors and embarrassing for island interpreters.

While living at the home of King Langlan in 1946, Eleanor had arranged to eat at the mess of the nearby navy post on Laura. This relieved the parishioners of the burden of providing her food; their resources were meager until the breadfruit trees were bearing again. But one day—she had been back in the islands only a short time—King Langlan had formally invited her to dinner and she had accepted. The invitation was brought by Barmi, the stout good-natured wife of Isaiah, the king's nephew. Eleanor assumed that dinner was at high noon. When she arrived, she found the king already eating in his small screened dining room. She was much surprised, for this was against all island custom to eat before a guest arrived. Moreover, the king was eating biru, which would never be offered to an American. Biru is made from the fermented breadfruit that has rather "gone by" after weeks or months of being buried in the earth. There was no deepfreeze to keep it fresh. So far as refrigeration was concerned, 1946 was just like 1846 or 1746 at Laura, Majuro Island. The "dug-up" breadfruit was washed in salt water and then in fresh, after which it was kneaded into small cakes or biscuits. These in turn were wrapped in breadfruit leaves and baked on hot stones buried in a pit. In Micronesia, this underground oven is called an um; in Polynesia, it is an imu. Only off-islanders who like strong cheese and whose olfactory organs are defective could really face a plateful of biru with equanimity. Long practice had made Eleanor accept whatever food was offered her with a smile of appreciation. She called on her reserves of courage and bit manfully into her cake of racy biru.

The king shared this food with her with perfect grace, showing no embarrassment. But why was there a look of astonishment on the face of Barmi when she brought in the plates? Surely Barmi herself had invited her to dinner!

The king looked at her and smiled. Islanders, a famous anthropologist in Honolulu had told her, needed no language to read the heart. She had the embarrassing feeling that he understood her dilemma and was trying to put her at her ease. Her Marshallese was limited; his English equally so. Yet he found suitable words with which to address her.

"You nejio (my child); I your papa."

He was telling her that she was as a child in his house. In any language, it was a gracious thought. So from that day she was "Nejio" to the old king, and he was "Papa."

She had just returned from a five o'clock supper at the Navy mess when she found Barmi waiting for her. She said politely, "Now is the time for dinner." She held out her hand to lead her guest to her uncle's eating house.

Eleanor was aghast. She had come one meal too early! She blushed to think of the embarrassment she had caused them. How was she to eat an island feast—her second supper —which, without doubt, the women of the household had been preparing all afternoon in the hot sun, over the hot stones of the um in the cookhouse? There was nothing else she could do.

She sat at the table and ate with the family—old King Langlan, his young wife and child, and his nephew, Isaiah. Barmi served. There was pig—the word pork is not in use in the islands; breadfruit and taro; and a pudding made from the center of the sprouted coconuts. It occurred to her that many an American hostess might have been less gracious if a guest had made the same mistake and come too soon.

Weddings, feasts, and funerals—they were all part of the life of an island missionary, quite as much as being tossed about in a canoe or sailing vessel wondering when and if one would make port.

Memories of Majuro—how many of them flooded back as she sat here on the porch of her familiar house in the year of Grace, 1950! Some of them were tragicomic. The worst of these was the time she had nearly been sent home for "misconduct."

That had been in 1946 shortly after her return to the islands, when things were still on a near wartime basis. Even after this lapse of time she could hear the words of a Navy man from Kwajalein who had come to Majuro to deliver an astonishing ultimatum.

"Miss Wilson," he had blurted out, "I have come to tell you that you are to be sent home!"

Eleanor had stared at him, not quite believing her ears.

"I! Sent home?" she exclaimed, utterly dumfounded at this blunt pronouncement. "On what charges?" It had been a long time since anyone had assumed such an attitude toward her or addressed her in such a tone of voice, and she was at a loss how to answer.

She studied the man. Except for his complete lack of diplomacy, he seemed in no way outstanding. Neither tall nor short, dark nor light, young nor old. Then she saw on the collar of his shirt the insignia of the chaplain's corps. But there was in his manner nothing to mark him as a man of the cloth, that invisible quality that attaches itself to those whose lives are dedicated to the service of their fellow men. His good opinion of himself was, however, quite adequate to shield him from any slightest compunction at being the bearer of such tidings. Perhaps the tropic sun had given him a slight case of megalomania.

"You know well enough on what charges!" he snorted. "Why, for shaving girls' heads, of course!"

"Shaving girls' heads!" Eleanor exclaimed. "Why would anyone do such a thing?"

"For breaking the Seventh Commandment!" He glared at her for a moment and then added with some heat, "And for stopping the Navy dances! It is no business of yours to interfere with the recreation of our Navy boys on duty in these islands. So *you* are to be sent home!"

"This is preposterous! I have never even seen a girl with a shaved head in all my years in Micronesia. You have been misinformed, Chaplain!"

If her voice lingered on the title, he did not choose to notice it. Eleanor went on more slowly, "The story has no grain of truth in it. Nor have I ever stopped a Navy dance. How could I, a missionary, do that?"

"You told your church members that if they let their girls attend the Navy dances they would lose their church membership, didn't you?" he demanded truculently.

"Chaplain," she said courteously and with an attempt at patience, "the Congregational Church, of which I am a minister, does not forbid dancing to its members. Apparently you do not know that the Marshall Island Churches are no longer under our jurisdiction, but are entirely independent of us. You must be new in these islands or you would surely have learned that the rules of the churches here are much more severe than ours at home, particularly in the punishment of any infraction of the moral law, which you say was the supposed cause of this 'incident.' As to the dancing, I did suggest to the mothers that if they did not wish their daughters to be disciplined by their own churches, they would do well to keep them home from the Navy dances. It was not a matter of my personal opinion regarding dancing. It was to avoid trouble for these young women —that was all. I have no authority over these people. I am here purely in an advisory capacity. I do not believe that any island girl has had her head shaved but I will make careful inquiry to find what could have given rise to such a story."

The chaplain was unconvinced. It takes a big person to admit gracefully that he is in the wrong and to attempt to make amends. Apparently the chaplain was not this sort of person.

He turned abruptly and went off to the village to pursue his investigation. Strong in authority and backed by a uniform that commanded local respect, he "interrogated" both the magistrate and scribe of the village. The shocked look on the faces of these island officials was not lost on him. He found only two "character witnesses" for the accused.

Being a stranger, he could not guess how swiftly word of his errand spread on the winds of rumor. As he walked back to the shore, the way was lined with onlookers. He smiled. No answering smiles greeted him. He was aware of covert, even hostile glances on the horrified faces of the elderly. He felt an uncomfortable prickle along his spine. And worse, as he passed one island home, a ripple of suppressed laughter reached him. A pretty young girl peered at him from the shadows, as if he were on exhibit, an oddity not to be missed. He could not be sure he was the cause of the giggling, but he had the uneasy feeling that he had cut a ludicrous figure here on Majuro. It was not an auspicious beginning for a future career, if there was one for him, in these islands.

It took some days for Eleanor to find out what had given rise to the story. Where there was so much smoke, there had indeed been a little fire. A Marshallese girl had been sent home from a certain island on this atoll by the U.S. Navy authorities as "an immoral woman." Her uncle, who was her guardian, had bobbed her hair as a punishment! Gone was the crowning glory of glossy black, the pride of every island girl. It has been a matter of family discipline in which neither church nor missionary had been involved.

There had been no apology, but Eleanor had stayed. She remembered the aftermath of the head-shaving incident, to her own embarrassment. She still blushed when she remembered it. Shortly after the visit from the chaplain, here in this very house, she had discovered unwelcome visitors in her hair. There had been nothing to do but bob it, so she could wash it daily. She could not imagine submitting to the monkeylike process of having a woman pick her head to find the intruders, so she had asked a girl to cut her hair. The girl had been abashed at such an unusual request, and had not been able to do it, so Eleanor had done it herself, and a very ragged job she had made of it. She then asked help in trimming it from an island boy named Kojrak, who was cutting his father's hair.

"Will you cut the back just as you did your father's and leave the front long?" she requested.

"O.K., Mother Wilson, O.K.," Kojrak beamed. He liked playing barber. It gave him a sense of importance.

Kojrak wielded his clippers. They weren't too sharp, and he had to give them a push. The first push plowed a path up to the top of her right ear! It was useless to scold him, for the damage was done. In the end she had come out looking like a gray-haired edition of a Japanese doll. But the "visitors" had been routed. She did not look pretty, but her head was clean.

The next day she had been mortified by an unexpected

visit, not from the chaplain, fortunately, but from the Commodore and his wife, from Kwajalein. She had kept her face toward them during their entire stay. *What* would they think, after the gossip there must have been in Navy circles, if they saw a smoothly shaved patch on the back of a missionary's head? They were cultivated people, and it was not difficult to explain to them the incident of the girl whose locks had been cut short, and of the churches' strict attitude toward dancing.

"I see," the Commodore said courteously. "It is not, then, that dancing offends the mores of Boston and the Mission Board, but of the islanders themselves. Well, we cannot very well question that rule, if it is a part of their religious belief."

"I am sure you do have a hard time providing proper social life for the Navy men," Eleanor said with understanding. "We do not mean to make it more difficult. But would you think it wise, Commodore, to subject our island girls so suddenly to a freedom and way of life for which they are totally unprepared? For the young men, their stay here is short. The girls must go on living in this community, where public opinion is a matter of much graver concern than any American can realize. You may guess its weight when you observe how well it serves to police islands where technically there is no law. A girl who loses her standing as a church member might find it hard to marry well. If she forms an attachment for an American, it is apt to have a most unhappy ending for both young people and their families and to create grave problems, not only for the missionaries but for the Navy authorities."

"Of course, Miss Wilson. I understand. Thank you for clearing up the matter."

And that had ended the matter of punishment for a "morals charge." Eleanor wondered with a wry sense of humor what would happen if the rules of the Marshallese churches regarding marriage, divorce and extramarital relationships were enforced in the U.S.A. It was the twentieth century on Beacon Hill, but it was still the 1850's in these islands! Eleanor had learned that one must sit back and let the island Christians themselves judge what was best for their own people. She could only advise, comfort the weak, help the afflicted and teach the age-old truth, that there is no happiness gained by harming another—which is, after all, the basic truth underlying all the "Thou shalt not" commandments. Once, she had been gravely shocked by the crudities of life with which she had been forced to deal, but experience had brought tolerance, and tolerance, compassion. How would we react, she wondered, if we were forced to adopt overnight the rules and customs of a society utterly dissimilar to our own? She felt sure that Christians of twentieth-century America would do well if they could live up to island standards. For almost a hundred years the word of God had been preached in these islands. Before that there had been only the worship of spirits, good and evil, of stones inhabited by nature gods, of the taro plant that gave them sustenance. The old legends had not met the people's needs. They had hungered for something more. They had found it in the teaching of the Boston missionaries of 1857 and to that rock they clung. She dared not by any word or action loosen their hold upon it.

Once she had gently tried to convince them that a man or woman should not be put out of the church for smoking, drinking or moral offenses, that they should rather be encouraged to see themselves as God saw them, to repent quickly and sincerely, and to return speedily to the church, which was the household of God.

"Mother Wilson," the dignified president of the Association of Marshall Island Churches said firmly, "Why do you bring up these questions which you do not understand?"

At first she was aghast at being so rebuked. Then she realized that perhaps they did understand their problem much better than she. For people not long out of heathenism, perhaps the very strictness of the "initiation rules" of the new order had made a strong appeal to the island psyche.

It was something clear-cut to live by. Perhaps, Eleanor hesitated to call them so, these were a new set of tabus. At all events, she was overruled. Even the respect in which they held their missionary could not sway them. She was in fact gratified for it meant that these people had come of age and could and would settle their own problems.

Of these, divorce was one of the knottiest. Uliga, Navy headquarters on Majuro Atoll, had become under American rule the "Reno of the Marshalls." A Marshallese, refused a divorce by the civil council members of his home atoll, all of whom were as a rule strict church members, could now appeal to higher authority at Uliga. The problem of the illegitimate child, under a matriarchal system, was not so serious as in other societies. It in no wise caused ostracism to the mother and left no stain upon the child. The child belonged as a matter of course to the mother's family and inherited his right to food and land through her. If the girl was young, her mother or an aunt took the baby, and no more was thought about it unless, and this was a very large unless, the family was composed of church members. Eleanor had married couples with children, as the head of the family set his house in order. No islander, however, was capable of such cruelty as was practiced among Anglo-Saxons. There were in the islands no Hester Prynnes.

Adoption was a widespread practice through all the islands. Its ramifications baffled even a person as long resident in the islands as their career missionary. Even in the best families, it was quite common to give an infant to a childless relative upon that relative's request. If one brother had five daughters, and another only sons, a daughter could be spared to brighten the other home. The child did not lose one set of parents, but gained another and visited freely between both homes. Indeed, when an islander said he wished to go and visit his mother, there was no way of knowing whom he meant. It might well be an aunt, for the Marshallese have no word for aunt. Any woman of their mother's clan and generation was called mother. This was all very strange to a proper Bostonian.

Sitting on her porch at Laura, other memories came to her—many of a solemn and religious nature, such as the celebration of the communion here back in January of 1947, at the close of an Association Conference. Twenty-five new members had been received into the church. She had then asked Barton, the local evangelist, to read the name of members of the Association who had died since the last conference in 1939 before the outbreak of the war. How startled she had been to hear not a single name of the deceased but only names of the living.

"But those people are not dead, Barton!" she had exclaimed. "I spoke with some of them only yesterday."

"They are dead in sin, Mother Wilson," Barton said stoically. "The others live, because they died in Christ."

She gasped. Church discipline in the Marshall Islands was something to be reckoned with. These former members might have been dropped for breaking a major commandment or for no more heinous offense than smoking.

The islanders' explanation of this seemingly harsh rule was simple. The Bible taught that the body was the temple given us by God to dwell in. It was as wrong to smoke in it as to smoke up the walls of a church. Therefore, it was not a light offense in island eyes.

Sin was a word that had gone out of fashion back in Boston about the time when "church clothes" had been relegated to mothballs—gone with the Prince Albert and the striped trousers, now the uniform of the diplomat and the undertaker. It was as antiquated as the horse and buggy. Since Freud, people were only frustrated when their "guilt complexes" caught up with them.

But in the islands the hard teaching of the mid-nineteenth century still stood. If one broke the law, punishment was swift and inevitable. There was an inflexible rule that no pastor, deacon, or committeeman might hold church office if the affairs of his household were not above reproach. The leaders must set an example to their people—a rule in all societies, both primitive and advanced. Eleanor, therefore, quite understood the embarrassment of a deacon who came to her after church to ask if his daughter might not be married that afternoon. He hastened to explain that there had been no minister on the atoll and. . . . He stammered a little and then went on.

"My daughter and my son-in-law have twins. It is most necessary, Mother Wilson, that the marriage take place at once."

He looked apprehensively at the lady missionary. He saw no criticism on her face or in her manner.

"I must first talk with the young people," she said gently. "If I feel that they truly wish to make this a Christian marriage, I will, of course, perform the ceremony this afternoon."

She was quite satisfied with their intentions. The girl was lovely and, by all accounts, had chosen a young man well thought of by their neighbors. The couple had lived with the girl's parents. Both were anxious to be reinstated as church members. It was decided to hold the wedding right after the Christian Endeavor Meeting, when most of the congregation of the Laura Church would be assembled.

"That will give you only a few hours for preparation," Eleanor warned the bride.

But the girl was beaming with happiness. This was a secondary matter, important as a wedding costume and flowers are to an island girl. They must be dressed in white in the American manner, no matter of what material the wedding dress may be made. Many an island bride has used white mosquito netting. And a veil is the sine qua non of every island wedding. Flowers grow by the wayside and the bright bougainvillaea, fragrant plumeria, or the ever-present hibiscus make the bride's bouquet and wreaths for the heads of her attendants. The bride had her veil and some bougainvillaea blossoms were stitched to the skirt of her cotton dress. The bridegroom was resplendent in white duck trousers, a dark blue coat and a large, paper boutonniere.

Eleanor made the service as lovely as she could. Her heart went out to the girl. Eleanor was sure her vows were quite as acceptable as many made under less duress before banks of orange blossoms at a cathedral altar while the soft tones of an organ filled the sanctuary. Here there was no music but the sound of the surf breaking on the shore only a few yards away.

It was customary to have a feast after a wedding, but at such short notice could one be contrived? Yet as they were making their way to the bride's house, savory odors reached the nostrils of the wedding party. The yard of the house was already the scene of activity, and down the path came two women with a long basket of coconut fronds hung on a pole laid over their shoulders. They set it down on the porch floor and out of it came a roast chicken, fresh bananas and breadfruit which had been roasted over an open fire. The charred skin of the breadfruit had then been scraped away, leaving a brown inner crust. There is no way to tell an off-islander what it resembles in taste. It is delicious in any form—baked, roasted, boiled or fried. It is like life in the islands—it must be experienced to be understood. All of the food, Eleanor learned, was the gift of King Jitiam, the lesser king of Majuro Island.

Jitiam had died in the fall of 1947, more than a year after her return to the Marshalls. Poor Jitiam had been dropped from the rolls of the church for the offense of smoking. The rules made for commoners applied equally to kings in perfect democracy. But some months before he died, he had given up tobacco that he might regain his membership.

Eleanor had been feeding the hens in her yard about her two-room house when she saw a great crowd gathering on the beach. Had a ship been sighted? None was expected. The people were gathered about something on the sand. Perhaps some fishermen had brought in an especially good catch. Leisurely, she had walked down to see.

"What is it?" she called.

"It is Jitiam!" an islander cried excitedly. "They have found him dead on the sand. He was just going out in his canoe."

There was Jitiam, his body crumpled as he had fallen to the beach, one hand reaching out toward his canoe that was beside him. He was an old man and had been for some time in rather poor health, so no one was much surprised. A group of his relatives came. They lifted him gently and carried him to the house of a neighbor, where they could prepare the body for burial. Funerals cannot be delayed long on equatorial islands. Preparations for interment must be swift.

Eleanor saw she was not needed. Her first thought was for the widowed queen, Lijamer. She was not in the crowd, but a woman said she had been told. Nor was she in her house. Where would she be? Eleanor thought but a moment. In all likelihood, she would go to the house of Mary Heine Lanwi. She found her there. Mary was talking quietly to her, and there was no trace of hysteria in the old woman's face or manner. She welcomed Eleanor with a grateful smile. Evidently they had been expecting her. Eleanor had grown accustomed to the placid acceptance of death by all the Marshallese. Like the first Christians in pagan Rome, they regarded death as a departure for a better world. But she was not quite prepared for the Queen's reaction to the results on earth of the King's sudden departure.

"Mother Wilson! How glad I am that you have come! Please stay with me! I am afraid of Jitiam's sister!"

The queen was a tiny person; her eyes, deep with sorrow, were round now with actual fear.

"She will come to my house and make trouble!" the Queen whispered.

Eleanor had heard that the sister had gone a little queer, and she quite understood the queen's uneasiness. Eleanor invited the queen to come and stay in her home until the body was laid out in the church. There, surrounded by relatives and friends, she need have no fear of the old woman's peculiarities. Eleanor was a little startled, when she was alone that night, to have the aged sister come knocking on the wall of her house, crying, "Jitiam! Jitiam!" like a witch's incantation in the darkness. It had given Eleanor quite a turn. She only hoped the old woman had mistaken the house and had not been troubling the queen.

"What must be done before the funeral?" she asked, knowing the value of hand-work in times of mental distress.

"Jitiam's white suit must be pressed. He was always very particular about it!" There was a quaver in the queen's voice.

"I will press it," Eleanor said.

But the pastor's wife, who had just come in, said that was a task she could do. When it was finished, she carried the pressed suit carefully to the house where the men were laying out the body of the dead king.

That funeral for some reason remained peculiarly vivid in Eleanor's memory. She could shut her eyes and see Jitiam's body laid out on two benches in the little church. A mat had been placed beneath it and a sheet over it. A wreath of sweet-scented papaya blossoms had been placed about his head, and another garland was draped across his chest. At first glance, the old king appeared to be asleep.

All his friends and followers came to the church to see him. It was not a sad time. Baby sitters are unknown at Laura, and the babies came, too, and played on the floor. One little boy leaned toward Jitiam and rested his elbow on the bench as he watched the woman who was fanning the dead king with the leaf of a breadfruit tree. Flies had already begun to gather. The fans were busy all day and all night, passing from one willing, brown hand to another.

Queen Lijamer sat quietly by Jitiam's head. How would she stand the ordeal of watching for a day and a night, as was the custom? Eleanor had insisted that she have coffee and a bite to eat before the ordeal began.

By late afternoon the coffin was ready. It had been made by loving hands and elaborately decorated. Its arched top

bore the painted words in English letters, but in the Marshallese language, "Yokwe Kom," meaning "Good-bye." It
was as if Jitiam were merely saying good-bye to his friends
before he left for a long journey.

The *wake* was interrupted by the sound of a motor out
on the lagoon. That could mean only that the coast guard
boat from Rong Rong was drawing up to the dock. Four
young Coast Guardsmen came ashore, carrying another
coffin on their shoulders. With them was Lieutenant Doster,
their commanding officer.

This posed a real dilemma. Which coffin should be used?
There was low talk in the back of the church as the pastor
and the deacons conferred. The coffin his own people had
made was more elaborate and more fitting for a king, but it
had been very kind of the Coast Guard officer to have a
coffin made for Jitiam. To offend him would have been unthinkable. With characteristic island courtesy, it was decided
that Jitiam would wish them to use the one the officer had
sent. So the royal coffin was put aside. It was used a few days
later for a commoner who died, little expecting to be buried
in the coffin of a king.

There were evening prayers that night in the church, and
then the sleeping mats were brought in. Some people slept,
while others kept watch. It was a solemn occasion, seen by
the light of two old kerosene lanterns in the front of the
church. But there was no silence. All night long the people
sang, one group taking up the hymn as the other grew
weary. The old Queen watched, her head drooping.

Next day, Eleanor read the funeral service. The old words
sounded especially meaningful as she saw the look of rever-
ence and hope on the faces of the church people. They
were glad that Jitiam had died a church member. It would
have been lamentable if he had not died in Christ. Many
spoke of his good life, his great kindness, his good deeds.

"Let not your heart be troubled . . ." Eleanor read the
words that had brought comfort to millions of listeners. "In

my Father's house are many mansions. . . ." "I am the resurrection and the life."

Last of all she read a passage from the twenty-third psalm:
"Yea, though I walk through the valley of the shadow of death, I will fear no evil: for thou art with me. . . ."

Then the man in charge of the funeral rose and said, "It is now time to bid Jitiam farewell."

This was the signal for general weeping. It lasted perhaps five minutes and stopped as suddenly as it had begun. After a few farewell remarks, everyone on Laura, it seemed, came to file past the dead king for the last time. Gifts were laid in the coffin—gifts curious to western eyes. These consisted of soap and money, two scarce items on Majuro Atoll. Afterwards they were taken from the coffin and distributed among the relatives. When all had passed, the six pallbearers carried the heavy plywood coffin, covered with a white cloth, to the little cemetery at the end of the island. One man followed behind the cortege, carrying the coffin lid, thus reducing its weight, for Jitiam was a heavy man.

The grave was not yet dug; this is the island custom. The coffin was set down on the sand, and the men began to dig. On a coral atoll, it took only a short time to dig down six feet. Now and then they turned up a bone that had dropped into the hole from an adjoining grave. It made Eleanor think of Hamlet. Space is narrow on an atoll, and graves must be dug very close together. At last it was ready. The lid was nailed on the coffin, and it was lowered on coconut fronds into the trench of sand. Then a final prayer was offered. Each villager threw in a little earth. The gravediggers covered the coffin with sand, and while others shoveled in the remaining sand, they stamped it down with their boots.

This was scarcely done before the piping of sandpipers was heard and a flock of these little brown birds circled in from the shore, as if some messenger had told them of the new mound in the sand. The Marshallese resolutely turned their heads away. These Kweleej birds were birds of ill omen, harbingers of ill fortune, haunters of graves. There was no naturalist to tell them that these birds sought nothing more than insects whose burrows had been disturbed by the digging of a grave.

Six days later, when the period of mourning was over, girls and women strung a neat rail of sennit cord to stakes driven about the old king's grave. Gifts were hung here as a part of the funeral observance. Later these were taken down and given to the family living under Jitiam's house. By this time the king's subjects had made a cement gravestone, into which had been cut the king's name in even, block letters. The workmanship would have done credit to a professional stone carver. This marker was placed upright at the head of the grave. Now fresh flowers were placed before the headstone in soda pop bottle vases. This was the final ceremony performed for Jitiam. The solemnity of it was broken by Jitiam's sister, who tried to take a lei from the sennit cord, and, not succeeding in this, sat down on the tombstone and plucked blossoms from the pop bottles, strewing them in the wind!

"Sweet bells out of tune," Eleanor thought. Denmark and island atoll had much in common, both in life and death.

Jitiam's sister was a weird figure, lean and gaunt. She could well have cried a warning to Macbeth from the dark heath. No one cared to stay with her. Something pre-Christian made the island people avoid her. Mental illness is rare in the islands, and there is no way to treat those afflicted with it. There are some cases of mental retardation, even of "queerness," but violent insanity seldom occurs. Eleanor attributed this to the lack of economic pressure in the present, and to the islanders' inability to worry about the future.

Members of the queen's family would stay with her for weeks to come. By then, doubtless the poor sister-in-law would have forgotten her present ill will, if such she harbored against the king's widow. The old king had gone to his reward. Now life on Majuro would go on as usual.

CHAPTER XII

A Summer of Peregrination

THAT SUMMER OF 1950 the *Morning Star VI* was a familiar sight in the waters about the Ratak and Ralik chains of the Marshall Islands. From Likiep to Aur Atoll, from Arno to Imroij, from Jaluit to Kwajalein, the *Star,* borne by the wind, sailed among the many islands of Eleanor Wilson's parish. Ailinglaplap saw the *Star,* and all over the island chains it was told with expressions of wonder how a woman was now captain of the mission ship. There was shaking of heads among old seafarers, but the women exchanged pleased glances. Perhaps there was nothing a woman could not do as well as a man, if she set her mind to it. Island women were expert canoe paddlers. Why not then master of a ship, now that all learning could be had from books? At Wotje, a crew of women sailed Eleanor out on the lagoon and set her proudly aboard the *Morning Star.*

"We can man a boat, too," they said.

New Bibles, hymnbooks and schoolbooks, magazines and pictures found their way to remote islets where the old ones had been worn to shreds by much use. Boxes of soap, a rare and needed item, reached the farthest outposts of the chains. And everywhere opportunity offered, Eleanor set up her kerosene projector and showed pictures, bringing to the islanders scenes from other atolls, the pictures of their friends, and Bible scenes to make vivid the well-known stories. The effect of all this on the morale of these communities could scarcely be overestimated. They were in touch with the world again. From the tops of tall coconut trees, Marshallese boys watched for the *Star* and spread the word of her approach.

And aboard the *Star*, the lady skipper felt a growing confidence. What was this sea sense that had to be learned, that no book could impart? She watched Mejjon at the wheel and began to "feel" when they approached land, though she saw small difference in the wave patterns that were so clear to him. She did take particular note of the flight of birds and soon learned that there were land-based birds, like the frigate bird, the brown booby gannet and the noddy tern, which always returned to land at night. That meant they could never be more than a day's flight from land. She found a copy of a little paper handbook put out during the war by Dr. Kenneth Emory of Bishop Museum, Honolulu. It was a pocket-sized book that seamen and fliers had carried on Pacific missions, a book that saved the lives of many an American. Here was the guide: A noddy tern was never seen more than twenty miles from land. He was a bird to watch for. In the late afternoon he would be winging toward his land base. The brown booby gannet might be seen thirty miles from shore. The white tern was not so good a guide, as he flew a hundred miles from his island base. Eleanor resolved to keep a sharp lookout for noddy terns, little brown birds with a gray spot on their heads. They were as good as channel markers. But always her main dependence was on the sextant and her watch that she wound with religious regularity.

Not all a missionary's life, however, is high adventure. Much of it is filled with endless, homely tasks, and some of it involves heavy labor. The most crying need in rebuilding the missions was for lumber. New lumber was not to be had; they must salvage old wherever they could. Coconut wood was useless for building because of its structure. And who would be so reckless as to cut down a breadfruit tree which provided the islanders' basic food? So the *Star* sailed back and forth from Roi, an abandoned Navy post of Kwajalein

Atoll, taking salvaged lumber to the Coast Guard cutter that lay off Kwajalein Island. The Coast Guard Station was next door to Rong Rong Mission, and it was not out of their way to deliver it.

Also, students and teachers must be taken home to their own islands for the summer vacations and to "work islands" where no one lived, but where the workers went to make copra. Copra represented almost the entire income of the islanders and, luckily, drying it on frames or laid out on the ground in the sun was work that any laborer could do. There was a limited market for Trochus shell, the toplike shell from which the Japanese still make buttons, but this income was negligible. A few islanders found work on boats and others at the Navy posts and hospitals. But the basis of all island economy was the coconut. And now that the crop in the Carolines was threatened by the dreaded rhinoceros beetle, Eleanor worried. What would happen to her parishioners if their main source of income were destroyed? The greater dread was that some synthetic product would be found to replace coconut oil as a base for soaps and shampoos.

One day in July of 1950, the first summer of Eleanor's command, the *Star*, loaded with homeward bound students, set out on the relatively short journey from Majuro north to the Atoll of Aur. They left Rong Rong in mid-afternoon. The weather was fair and promised to continue so. Even Luckabudge saw nothing ominous in the clouds. Yet they had scarcely left their anchorage, heading for the narrow pass west of Iroij Island, when the sun disappeared and the wind began to blow hard. The air was murky and a steady drizzle set it. It was only eight miles from the mission to this pass, through which small ships might leave the lagoon of Majuro Atoll for the open Pacific. It was not until they came abreast of it that they felt the full force of the rising gale. The prevailing winds were from the northeast and now they were driving giant waves from the broad ocean straight through the pass into the lagoon. This was no longer a place of shelter, for its waters were as rough as the sea beyond the reef.

Eleanor sent the students below, but she remained on deck. She watched old Mejjon at the wheel, his hands knotted about the spokes. There was something of grandeur in the old man's aspect as he fought to keep the *Star* on her course. His head was pulled well into the hood of his black raincoat, but his eyes peered out, intently studying the waves. The rain seemed to have no effect on the giant rollers. He swung the wheel back and forth, holding her to the safest course.

"The wind is freshening, Mejjon," Eleanor called, as, clinging to the rigging, she made her uncertain way aft to join him. "Do you think we can make it through the western pass?"

"We'll see, Mother Wilson," he shouted back. Even as near as she was to him it was difficult to hear, for the wind caught his words and seemed to blow them over the port rail. Eleanor nodded, knowing she could safely trust to his judgment.

He peered through the mist at the faint outlines of the reef and seemed satisfied; and, as always, the confidence of the island captain communicated itself to his crew.

"We could go 'round to Calalin and anchor in its lee for the night," Eleanor shouted back to him. "Maybe it will clear by morning!"

Mejjon shook his head. He tried again and again to get through the pass, but each time wind and water drove them back. Without a glance at Eleanor, he called out "Riuk!" meaning to come about. The *Star* swung to the west, then to the south, beating back into the lagoon. There was only one thing they could do—round the Island of Iroij and, keeping well off the sand bar below it, come up into the shelter of the Point of Calalin. Iroij was a desolate, uninhabited island set between the two arms of the reef, leaving a pass on either side of it. Eleanor peered anxiously land-

ward. As they skirted the sand bar, Iroij was only a blob of
gray topped by swaying palm trees. The water was less
rough, once they made the shelter of the point, the eastern
boundary of the pass. The *Star* seemed to gather her strength
for the contest ahead. Plainly, Mejjon meant to try again
to make the open sea here through the pass northeast of
Iroij. The men were at their posts, waiting expectantly.
Boaz was at the forepeak on lookout.

"Clear ahead!" he called. His voice was thrown back by
the wind.

Mejjon leaned on the wheel as the *Star* was again buffeted
by the waves. All aboard her felt helpless as the rudder took
the beating of the sea and the ship was blown about at the
caprice of the wind. The *Star* heeled over until the deck was
at an angle of forty-five degrees to the sea. Yet it was not as
bad as before, for to starboard they had the shelter of the
point. This time they would make it, Eleanor thought. In
the other pass they were headed directly into the wind. Here
they could take it on their starboard quarter. Mejjon was a
master seaman. In a matter of minutes they were through
and headed directly north for Aur.

Yet there was small cause for rejoicing for the sea was in-
credibly rough. Eleanor wondered if she should have overruled Mejjon's decision and have ordered the *Star* laid to
off Calalin. It was one thing to risk her own life and that of
grown men, trained to the sea, and quite another to risk
those of the students entrusted to her care. But they had
been between Scylla and Charybdis, for it would have been
no easy night tossing about in the lagoon in constant peril
of being driven on the reef. A sailing vessel was infinitely
safer on the open sea. To a landsman, the land, any land,
seems to offer safety. To a seaman, when buffeted by the
winds and fighting heavy seas, land became a menace, and
his greatest fear is that he will be driven on a lee shore. For
him safety or relative safety lies in heading for the open
sea.

Yet the open sea had its own terrors. The *Star* fought the

waves which today seemed intent upon destroying her. There was something sinister about the thundering gray water that repeatedly swept over them. To Eleanor it seemed like the battle between Michael and Lucifer, the struggle of archangels.

She saw the intent look on Mejjon's face. It made her follow his glance. Her heart turned over. Coming directly toward them was a great wall of water. In that moment of stark terror, it seemed to tower higher than the mainmast itself. Her hands tightened in a death grip on the top of the gunwale.

The *Star* leaped like a frightened horse, then fell sickeningly sideways, while tons of water poured over her deck. Another wave, almost as high, was coming down on her, but they could not turn back now. Darkness had fallen, and no living thing but fish or porpoises could have gone through the pass in these seas without daylight. Oh, why had they not anchored in the lagoon? The lives of all aboard were in her keeping. But if they turned back every time there were rough seas, the *Star* would seldom leave any harbor! One had to have faith.

She thought of her students, all sick and terrified no doubt, below deck. She must go to them! She swallowed hard and made her way along the cockpit. It seemed to her the deck was nearly vertical. She lurched down the ladder and was hurled through the open door of her cabin. She caught at the side of the bunk to keep from falling.

All the six bunks were filled, if the limp forms of her girl students could be counted. They seemed more like bundles of clothing than the bright young girls who had stepped aboard the *Star* that afternoon, so gay and happy at the thought of going home to see their parents.

"All settled for the night?" Eleanor asked, trying desperately to keep her voice low and controlled.

Seven pairs of eyes, six girls and one little boy, were raised to her with the hurt look of dumb creatures whose confidence has been betrayed. There was no answer from the figures in the bunks, but a whimper came from the floor at her feet. Eleanor started. There on a pile of baggage rolls lay Togo, a little twelve-year-old boy, who had been so over-joyed at going home. He was the little boy who at first had been so homesick. He had come wailing to Eleanor, repeating over and over, "Elap ao brumoj!" meaning, "Great is my sorrow!" But he had soon recovered and was the merriest child at Rong Rong Mission School.

There was no merriment left in him now. He looked at her in helpless misery.

"Togo, don't you want to go in the main cabin with the boys? You would feel the motion of the ship less in there," she said.

He could only shake his head. One hand reached out and clutched her skirt, as if she, and only she, could give him any shred of comfort in his extremity.

"All right then, Togo, you may stay," she said gently. "I will put a bucket beside you, in case you need it."

"Mother Wilson, I am *so* sick!" a girl student wailed.

"I know, dear. But this will soon pass, and you will feel better tomorrow."

But right at this moment, to the mission students, tomorrow seemed as distant as eternity.

Sixty miles from Majuro to Aur! And due north all the way. But this night she could not go on deck to check their course. She must leave the sailing to Mejjon. His instincts were older and surer than her recently acquired knowledge. Once a teacher, one never loses the terrible urgency of caring for one's charges, and tonight the children were her responsibility. The ship was in Mejjon's trained hands; their lives in the hands of God.

That night was one of torment. Everything in the cabin seemed to be moving in a different direction. It took on a nightmare quality. It was to come back in her dreams for many months afterwards—the rising on the crest of the wave, and then the sickening downward plunge when it seemed the *Star* must be driven into the depths of the sea, taking them all with her. Then, as the wind screeched and the water pounded the hull, the ship would right herself and fight on, her timbers groaning in sympathy, it seemed, with the moaning of her sick and terrified passengers.

There was no longer any question whether Eleanor should go on deck. She could not, if she would, for the ship was pitching so violently, she could not have climbed the ladder. There was nothing to do but endure.

There was a sickening thud as something struck the Star's side! Was it another ship, some derelict, or a floating piece of wreckage? Would her seams hold? The dinghy—it would not hold even the children and one man to row—not half of those aboard. And how many minutes could a dinghy survive in such seas? There were life jackets enough, of course. She had seen to that. What chance was there of being picked up? Eleanor shut her eyes. Not that, dear Lord, not that!

Suddenly fragments of an old familiar poem came to her out of some hidden pocket of memory:

> We were crowded in the cabin,
> Not a soul would dare to sleep,
> It was midnight on the waters,
> And a storm was on the deep.

She could not remember all of it, only snatches.

> "We are lost!" the captain shouted,
> As he staggered down the stairs.

She recalled thinking, as a reader on dry land, that this was sheer melodrama. Somehow, when one was at sea in a tempest—yes, that was the name of the piece—it did not seem overdrawn at all.

> But his little daughter whispered
> As she took his icy hand,
> "Isn't God upon the ocean,
> Just the same as on the land?"

All the children were sick. The odor was revolting. A
sailor made his rounds between the boys' cabin and theirs,
emptying the buckets and bringing them back. She began to
pray. A sense of comfort came over her, and there was a
presence in the cabin that had not been there before. Suddenly Eleanor felt quite sure that they would ride out this
storm. Either the *Star* was pitching less, or she had grown
accustomed to it. Now and then, fitfully she slept. She
heard a tiny snore from the bunk opposite. One girl at least
was asleep. On the baggage roll, little Togo lay still.

By morning, the wind had abated somewhat. She woke to
that wonderful realization. The closing lines of the old
ballad came to her:

> And we anchored safe in harbor
> When the morn was shining clear

"Come, children," Eleanor said. "It is safe enough now to
go on deck. We will feel better in the fresh air."

The cabin still reeked in spite of the sailor's ministra-
tions, and she had to fight down her own nausea. She
climbed the ladder with her young and bedraggled flock
behind her. She felt rather like a ruffled mother duck as she
paddled across the deck to drop, rather than sit, on the roof
above the stair well. She smiled at Mejjon, who had been
relieved at the wheel by Boaz, but who still refused to go
below.

"Well done, Mejjon! Well done, all of you! You have
saved the *Star* and all our lives. I am proud of you!"

It was as if she had knighted them.

A sailor lowered a bucket over the side on a rope and
pulled it up full of salt water. They washed in it gratefully.
Indeed, this was the only way there was to wash aboard the
Star.

Now the boys came up from the main cabin. They looked
white and "peaked," as her grandmother would have said,
but not one was hurt.

With fair winds they would have been in sight of Aur

after an all-night sail. But before them was no hint of gray that might mark the presence of an atoll. Not a single bird was in sight. Had they been driven far off their course? All about them was only tossing gray water—water, water, everywhere, as in the tale of the *Ancient Mariner*. There must be millions of tons of gray water out there, and overhead hung gray rain clouds, ready to drop more upon them. And nowhere was there a single speck of land.

"What is our course, Freddy?" she called, for the demi-Scotsman was now at the wheel. Freddy shrugged. Not even a Frenchman could have conveyed more with a single gesture. It said as plainly as the moving, illuminated letters running around the Times Building in Times Square that he hadn't a ghost of an idea.

"We go north, Mother Wilson!" he grinned as he spoke. "Only north from where or to where, who can know? But we are afloat! Last night, I didn't know if I was ever to see Ebon Island and my home again." He glanced up scornfully at the lad in the rigging. "It is no use to look for land!" he said. "We are far, far off our course!"

"Maybe by afternoon we shall sight land," Eleanor told the students. "You must all keep watch."

There was nothing else to do and it would keep them occupied.

Mejjon came and stood beside her. Now that the storm had abated, she was again in charge.

"Which way shall we steer, Mother Wilson?" he asked.

For some reason she could not fathom, she was impelled to say, "West, Mejjon. I feel that Aur Atoll is to the west. We were driven too far east in the night. I could tell a little by the impact of the waves."

Mejjon sniffed the air. It somehow reminded Eleanor of pictures she had seen of Eskimo husky dogs sniffing the breeze.

"I think you are wrong, Mother Wilson. I believe Aur is to the east."

Eleanor considered. She could not justify her feeling.

Dead reckoning was useless after a night of being blown over the sea with no way to tell their speed or whether they were on course. She had better let Mejjon try his system of navigation.

"Very well, Mejjon," she said. "Try sailing to the east."

They had food and water, and for twenty-four hours at least few would want much food. No fire could be kindled in the galley stove, for it was still too rough. The very thought of food was revolting to most of the passengers. The crew, all hardened seamen, would break their fast on ship's biscuits, wet down with canned milk and liberally sprinkled with sugar. It would take more than a tempest to spoil an island seaman's taste for sweets!

They had been on an easterly course only an hour when one of the crew shouted, "Bao! Bao!" He pointed to a small gray bird riding unconcernedly on the waves. It rose, circled, and lighted on the gaff of the mains'l. It poised there a moment, seeming almost to have a fixed purpose. Then it rose and flew off directly west.

"Mejjon!" Eleanor cried. "It is flying west. You know that bird cannot fly too far from land! Land is to the west!"

"You are right, Mother Wilson," the sailing master said. He was silent a moment, then added in a low voice, "I think God spoke to you, and perhaps He sent the bird to guide us!"

The helm spun and the *Star* wheeled about. It took skill to get her on the other course. All heads ducked as the boom swung over. Then with the wind on her starboard quarter, the *Star,* like a little white tern at home on the water, headed, almost joyously it seemed, west for land, if not Aur, any land where the bird had its "land base." A shout went up from the crew and the mission children.

"I shall love birds all my life," little Togo said earnestly. "I shall not ever let any boy capture one. This one is our friend. I will be his."

"Good, Togo," Eleanor commended. "We must not forget at evening prayers to thank God for sending us a guide."

Togo nodded. He felt as if he were much older than twelve—almost a man. He would not cry next fall when he went back to school. Tears were for girls and babies. But they were not far below the surface right now.

Night fell, but the sky was overcast and no stars shone through. They could only trust and keep to their course a little north of west. At daybreak a crewman went aloft in the rigging, keeping a sharp lookout for land. It seemed as if they were all alone in the whole Pacific. No more birds appeared, nor a ship, nor did they hear even the distant droning of a plane.

At morning prayers, Eleanor could not help thinking what a dreadful calamity it would be if the mission ship were lost with all its crew and with the precious lives of the children committed to her care. It would be a setback to God's work that would take many years to overcome. It must not be!

She glanced at Mejjon. His face was perfectly calm. He trusted to his missionary, to their God and to His messenger. He did not believe they would be lost. About two in the afternoon, the lookout cried, "Land-o!" Not only was it land —it was the Atoll of Aur! They should be ashore in two hours. Eleanor felt weakness overcome her. Her young charges were safe! Wan faces smiled. Haggard students became suddenly alert. Little Togo gave just the note of comedy relief they all needed.

"Mother Wilson," he wailed. "I'm hungry! You didn't give me any breakfast."

Everyone howled with laughter. If anyone had offered Togo the choicest morsel—even the rare treat of a chocolate candy from one of the gift boxes that came to Eleanor at Christmas—he would have fled to the rail.

Bukmeto, the cook, roared. "I make no fire, now! You can have a banana or one of the Kusaie oranges, or a ship's biscuit. Which will it be?"

And soon everyone aboard was munching on biscuits and bananas. Eleanor slaked her thirst with one of the last precious oranges that a ship had recently brought them from her old home island far to the west. What a luxury they were, though green and woody compared to Florida or California fruit. The way things tasted was all a matter of time and place. Right now she could believe that it was an orange that gave rise to the legend of the golden apples of the Hesperides.

Soon they were safely anchored and had been ferried ashore by canoes. They were too weary and sick to have a welcoming party. Eleanor told their island hosts they must all rest and have water to drink and to bathe. Their skins were burned from the salt water that had soaked them on the voyage.

By evening they were all as good as new. They held a meeting in the great airy, thatched house on Aur. Aur had no pastor, so Eleanor conducted the meeting. She had her small portable screen and her kerosene-run slide projector, so they had "pictures," which were indeed magic lantern pictures to people living far from the land of the motion pictures and the television screen. She showed colored slides of the dedication of her school at Rong Rong a year before. There were rows of students sitting under the palms on coral stones, there were views of the dormitories, of Bourn's thatched house, and of the library that had been floated there on the kerosene drums from Majuro Island.

Every once in a while someone in the audience would recognize a friend or kinsman in the pictures.

"There is Elanjo!" a native of Aur cried in delight, as the picture of the music teacher of the mission came on the screen. Elanjo had supervised the building of the school and this had been a proud day for him.

Elanjo had made up an alma mater song and taught it to the students to sing at the dedication. There was no need for sound effects for the Rong Rong students present burst into song now as they saw Elanjo on the screen, his baton suspended in mid-air. And over the sandy atoll rang a tune that any college student in America would recognize. It was

"Far above Cayuga's Waters." How far away was "Fair Cornell!" But the children sang the old tune with as much gusto as any Cornellian, with the words of their own alma mater—Rong Rong Mission School.

The strain of the storm and its near disaster was forgotten. That was yesterday and this morning was gone into the infinity of time with other ills. This was tonight—they were safe, dry, well fed and happy, and they were having the time of their lives. They had come home to be treated with respect and honor by their relatives and kinsmen. They were the happiest home-returned students in all the world.

And to the islanders who had no pastor, it was a rare and signal honor to have their own missionary from Boston on their atoll. They could not go to the big world. But the world, at least the world of their own church, had come to them aboard the *Star* in the person of Miss Eleanor Wilson.

It was a joyous night on the sandy shore of Aur. Eleanor knew a sense of fulfillment—of deep content. It was for nights like these and the smiles on the faces of her parishioners that made all things worth suffering—even the risk of being lost forever on the trackless sea.

And still they clamored for more slides. It was such a rare treat, especially for the old people, that she could not refuse to run them while the kerosene held out and there was a slide left in the box.

"That's Lakabun!" an aged woman cried.

Lakabun lived more than two hundred miles away, but the old people all seemed to know him. Though none of these pictures had been taken at Aur, it was astonishing how many of the persons they knew. The miles of ocean between their islands were to this seafaring, canoe-wise people no more of an obstacle than a few miles of country road might be to a farmer back home.

How the girl students shouted when they saw themselves gathered about a huge kettle of rice which the boys had just brought from the cookhouse.

Eleanor showed them a few pictures of the Holy Land,

taken to show the route of Saint Paul on his great missionary journeys. Then it was time for refreshments. Coconuts were passed around and soon after everyone was ready for sleep.

The next day the *Star* sailed a few miles up the lagoon to Tabal, the largest village on the atoll. Here lived the widow of Carl Heine, the Australian missionary. She was his second wife, sister of his first wife, who had died in childbirth.

Eleanor came to her tiny clapboard house. Politely, as island custom demanded, she took off her shoes, inevitably stained from the coral soil. Kneeling in front of the old woman, she put out her hand and said, "Yokwe Yuk, Mrs. Heine."

A smile lighted the old woman's face, but there was none in her eyes, for the aged Mrs. Heine had gone blind.

"It is you, Mother Wilson!" she exclaimed with keen pleasure. "I heard you would come!"

This woman, Eleanor thought, was as near a saint as any mortal was likely to get. If the Congregational Church went in for saints, it would have been her due. She had contracted this blindness, not from any natural cause, but as a result of gonorrhea, contracted from a young mother whose child she had delivered. But there was not a trace of bitterness in the heart of the woman who had, with her marriage, given her life wholly to the Lord's work.

Eleanor expressed her sympathy for all the grief the old woman had endured—the loss of her husband, the disappearance of her stepson and his wife. The Japanese had not molested her, as she was a pure Marshallese, not a Caucasian. She spoke no English, and, as she had no eyes, she could not well spy upon them.

Eleanor marveled at the great spiritual strength this Marshallese woman possessed. Even as a girl she had not been one-half as beautiful nor as gifted as her sister. Indeed, she had been like Leah; her beautiful sister like Rachel. But she had grown in strength with the years and given her children one by one to the Lord's work.

With a curious native dignity, she dismissed her own

sorrows and asked about the work of rebuilding the missions. Then she spoke with pride of her children and grandchildren, of Bourn, of Mary and of Dwight. She had, she said, so much to be thankful for. She had reason to give thanks to God. And now that she was old, she could see His hand in all that had happened.

Eleanor felt there would indeed be golden slippers for this servant of God in a better world. She hoped they would not be heavy on feet that had worn no shoes in this life.

The *Star* stayed as long as it could. There was grief when they left. The visit had been a bright interlude in the monotonous lives of the people of Tabal. It would be talked over for years to come. But they had supplies for the missions at Maloelap and Wotje, which lay northwestward along the Ratak, or eastern, chain of islands. And the days would go swiftly and they must not fail to complete their summer's journeying and get the students back to Rong Rong in September. They waved good-bye and from the shore towels and handkerchiefs were waved as long as they could be seen from the deck of the *Star*.

CHAPTER XIII

Seasons and Holidays

AUGUST OF 1950 came and Eleanor, working over her line-a-day diary, realized she had been skipper for some six months and that without serious mishap. It gave her something of a start. Six months! And how much sea experience she had packed into that half year, short to some perhaps, but long enough to a sea officer without a license, or ticket as a merchant mariner would say.

Spring and summer had gone by and autumn was here. How keenly she missed the changing panorama of the seasons. At home in New England the fields would have changed from the first delicate green of April to the rich golds of ripening grain, and now they would be purple and gold with aster and goldenrod and the woods would be red with the flame of oak and maple leaves. Here on the equator there was no season, except for the shifting of the winds. It was always summer and although it had the look of a tropic paradise, there was about it a deadly monotony unknown to the temperate climates. The principal events that broke the round of a missionary's duties were the great feasts of the church year, Christmas and Easter; and now, since the Navy had come, the secular holiday of the Fourth of July. Then, too, each little island celebrated its own independence day on the date it was liberated from the Japanese.

In October the "Master" and crew of the *Morning Star VI* had the opportunity to be present at a ship launching, a notable event anywhere, and one of great jubilation in the islands. The people of Rongelap had bought an old Navy hull and had rebuilt it for carrying their copra to Kwajalein. They had to wait until a government boat or island trader stopped at their islet and, as they did not have adequate storage, some of their crop would surely spoil. Copra, oddly enough, cannot be allowed to get wet; it becomes combustible and might set off a fire. It was not easy to keep it dry in sheds without sides and with only thatched roofs. Now they would be able to carry it to Kwajalein, or rather to the tiny island town of Ebeye five miles away. There they could sell it and bring home flour, rice, sugar, canned goods, and soap—the articles most needed in their community.

What an occasion they made of the launching! The mast glistened with new paint. The sails had never yet felt the salt spray. All in all, the finished boat was a credit to a people who had once been famous canoe builders. For this occasion, as always, gifts were in order. The entire superstructure of the ship was hung with dress lengths of cotton goods, with shell-trimmed Marshallese baskets, feathered fans, finely woven mats, every sort of island handicraft. It would never do to launch a ship without gifts.

Even the commanding officer of Kwajalein was there and a Navy wife had a beribboned bottle to break against the prow. Just before the ship was shoved into the water, the gifts were taken down, and the dress goods given to the island people, the handicraft to the Americans. Then every able-bodied person—men, women, and children—caught hold of the boat's sides and helped run her into the water. They were waist-deep before she floated free. A roar went up from every throat. Eleanor thought of ship launchings at home. What was there about them that always gave the watcher a lifting of the heart? Was it the age-old sense of adventure in man, his glorying to try his strength against the mighty sea? She smiled, remembering the carved figureheads of New Zealand canoes she had seen—with the figure thrusting out its tongue in derision, that the gods of the sea might know he was unafraid.

At this launching she was not invited to share the trial run. She had been so "honored" when she had said the prayer for Lelej's canoe launching at Laura. She had been seated in the place of honor, the "deck," or platform, between the canoe and the outrigger. The sail had been hoisted and they were skimming merrily over the lagoon when there was a sudden ominous crack as the light mast gave way under the weight of the heavy tarpaulin they had used for a sail. Instantly the men grabbed it as the canoe careened crazily. She had hung on for dear life, much hampered by a dress length of print goods from some New England mill—one of the gifts presented to her for the occasion.

Eleanor determined to make her next stop Maloelap, an island that had had no visiting missionary for a long while. Sometimes, in performing the necessary workaday chores, the *Star's* primary purpose was of necessity set aside, that of being a floating parsonage to carry a missionary about her isle-set parish. At Maloelap, Eleanor brought out her official white robe, for this would be Communion Sunday. Usually this was celebrated quarterly but, as this island had no ordained pastor, it must of necessity be whenever the missionary could come. Moreover, it would be baptism Sunday as well, as it was customary to baptize babies at the time of the Communion observance.

The little church was made of wooden clapboards and could hold perhaps two hundred people. There were, of course, no pews. Everyone sat with ease and grace on the floor. Invariably the women sat on one side of the church and the men on the other. This day the church was filled. Everyone came whether or not he was a member in good standing, though only communicants partook of the sacred elements. These were perhaps a third of all the islanders. Church membership, being difficult to retain, was consequently cherished. It was not easy for the deacons to pass among the closely packed audience. Now and then a baby whimpered and was carried out by a little girl, the usual baby watcher. The mother remained in her place. Otherwise the atmosphere of solemnity was unbroken. To Eleanor, serving in this setting, the sense of the oneness of the Christian Church in all places and in all times was very real.

That afternoon, five little ones were baptized—all tiny infants. There are no godparents in a nonconformist church, but unofficial ones came forward to sponsor these children. These were aunts, uncles, and family friends. Every child had a full complement.

They had expected to hold a wedding but regretfully Eleanor had to decline. The young couple had neglected to obtain a marriage license when the scribe was on the island. Now he had gone and it was impossible to get one. Civilization with some of its irksome regulations had touched even the remote atoll of Maloelap.

It was October when she arrived at Rongelap, the nearest atoll to Bikini. Rongelap was celebrating its Jubilee. Just fifty years before, the first Christian missionary had come to this atoll. There was no seer to warn that some years hence these people would have to abandon their atoll, at least for a time, because of an atomic fall-out, due to a freak change in the winds that blew from the tests at their neighboring atoll of Bikini. But it was not a native of Rongelap who came out first to welcome the *Star* to the Jubilee celebration. A big crowlike bird had elected himself the welcoming committee and had come out to pilot the ship in. As they neared the shore, all aboard the mission schooner could hear singing. A large rowboat, holding some twenty islanders, was coming out to meet them. They were singing the *Morning Star* hymn, composed by one of the early missionaries.

> Iju Ran! Iju Ran!
> Kio ej walok jen rear;
> *Morning Star! Morning Star!*
> Itok kin emon; . . . .

Their voices carried for a great distance across the water. Every syllable was crystal clear. What singers they were! Music came as natural to them as breathing, and even the smallest children could make a three-part song out of almost nothing. They knew that music came from the heart and only long afterwards found its way into books.

> Jej monono wot ran in,
> Bwe ej walok Iju Ran;
> Iju Ran romak kio,
> Kemaramlok kij.
> (We are full of joy today
> Because the *Morning Star* appears;
> Morning Star shine now,
> Keep us in that light.)

On shore Eleanor could catch glimpses of the red dresses of the women and the straw hats of the men. Clearly everyone was dressed to the nines. Even the rowboat looked festive with the people waving a white flag to assure the strangers that they would not be killed, but welcomed as friends! This was something about which the first missionaries had needed much assurance. The boatmen were a part of the Rongelap Pageant. Eleanor could not help wishing she had a Mother Hubbard dress, ankle length or a little better, to look more like her predecessors. It was well today that she did not have on slacks! That would have been a scandal of awful proportions.

Then the islanders were swarming over the sides, and in the age-old manner offering the seafarers fresh drinking coconuts. They were the kind for which this northern atoll is famous.

The Jubilee was conducted with the greatest ceremony. They had relatively few great events to celebrate, and naturally this one called for their best efforts.

Eleanor and the guests of honor were seated at a table under a thatched roof of an open-air building. The eighty islanders squatted comfortably on the ground, eating their food from coconut fronds laid out on coral pebbles. There was roast chicken, beru cake made from arrowroot flour and pandanus, and giant doughnuts fried in pig grease. There was also a special treat for their missionary—a can of date-nut bread. Just how they had come by it was a minor mystery. The island children gathered around, wide-eyed, to watch her open it with the little key attached to the bottom. *This* was a strange way to get food. One tiny fellow did not believe it was really something to eat until he had seen the guests put it in their mouths. Eleanor cut it in as many pieces as possible, so that all at the tables might have a taste.

But the real fun began when the feast was over. Eleanor enjoyed herself as she had not done in months. The actors in the pageant had so far as possible discarded modern clothes. Gone were the Navy surplus khakis and old, blue dungarees. Bare-chested and with loin cloths or grass skirts, the actors threw themselves into their parts in a way that would have made a Hollywood camera crew grind frantically to get the scene. A young man sat on the ground beating on a drum made from a hollow coconut log with a sharkskin stretched over one end. The deep, intermittent tone of the drumbeats set the tempo for the play. Over at one side, a group of men of Rongelap pushed into the clearing a boat made of canvas. The modern touch was that it ran on wheels! The boat even had a mast and clearly it was meant to represent the ship of the first missionaries who came to Rongelap fifty years ago. It had taken nearly fifty years after the coming of the first missionaries to Micronesia for Christianity to reach this remote northern atoll of the Marshalls. These missionaries were not white men with Bibles, shown in the usual missionary pageant, but Marshallese who had become Christians and now had set out to convert their fellow islanders.

At this point the drumbeats grew louder. The tempo was stepped up. The blood of the listeners coursed faster. There was a definite feeling of increased suspense. When the drum-

beat had become almost unbearable, out of the trees rushed
two brown men waving ironwood spears. One man had on
a grass skirt, the other, a small woven mat secured fore and
aft to his belt. But the latter had been too modest to take off
his trousers and had only rolled them up! These, with his
G.I. boots, were the false notes in the scene of primitive
onslaught. The spear waving had been realistic enough! The
doughty Marshallese missionaries, however, did not give an
inch of sand! They stood by their boat singing hymns until
they drowned out even the sound of the throbbing drum.
Then the grass skirt, the spears and the drum were thrown
in a heap, discarded forever. There was no further need of
them. It had been a short skit, but in a few brief moments
it had told the often repeated story of the gradual conquest
of the new over the old, of the gospel over pagan custom.

That afternoon in the church there was group singing.
An old man rose and explained the words of each song before it was sung, for the songs and chants were in the language of their ancestors, much of it unintelligible to the people of today. Pictures had been drawn, and when they were
uncovered, the islanders sang. One was of a ship lost at
sea, guided to land by a tiny bird and by the presence of
a certain fish. It was an old, old story, this problem of making one's way across the sea among these scattered isles.
Eleanor thought of the bird that had guided them safely to
Aur.

It was a two-day celebration. Jubilees do not come every
year. This one would be long remembered. Eleanor brought
ashore a gift of a large sack of flour, only to receive one in
turn, and a bag of rice besides. HOW could she ever repay
the islanders' generosity! Out of their little, they gave so
much! When it was time to leave, everyone of all ages came
down to the shore. The large rowboat was waiting to take
Eleanor and her crew back to the *Star,* anchored far out on
the lagoon.

She offered a farewell prayer. As the rowboat was shoved

off from shore, with one accord the people broke into song:
"God be with you till me meet again!"

Eleanor's eyes were wet. She was not getting any younger.
Not many more years, and she would be retired. Would she
ever see the parishioners of Rongelap again? It made the
parting extraordinarily touching. It was hard to join in,
but she tried. Yet no Anglo-Saxon voice is like the deep-
throated tones of the Marshallese. Over the water came the
chorus:

> Till we meet!
> Till we meet!
> Till we meet at Jesus' feet;
> Till we meet! . . . .
> Till we meet!
> God be with you till we meet again!

Like an autumn leaf the *Star,* blown by winds now favorable, now contrary, made her way from Rongelap to Kwajalein, from Kwajalein to Likiep, from Likiep to Rong Rong
in Majuro Atoll, her home port. From Rong Rong they
went to Imroij, arriving late in December, just in time for
the dedication of the new church. With Eleanor on the *Star*
went an octet of students from Rong Rong School to sing
the special song they had learned for the occasion.

It was just before Christmas. The solemn dedication must
be first for Christmas was a happy time of much singing, and
the church must be free for this long awaited day, the high
light of the church year. Eleanor had spent many Christ-
mases in the islands but this dedication had a special meaning for her, perhaps because of the trepidation with which
she had undertaken her first voyage there. Without the *Star,*
there would have been no lumber for the church that was
now the pride of the atoll.

It had taken the people of this island only a few months
to build the neat, board church from new lumber and the
salvaged roofing the *Star* had brought from Kwajalein Atoll.
Eleanor's heart swelled as she looked at it, with the warm

sense of seeing a task well done, a task in which she had had some part. From the vantage point of many months of skippering the *Star* she could look back with amusement at her fears on that first trip. She recalled the laying of the buoy a few seconds before the plane's arrival. Well, her raw apprenticeship was over. She could now consider herself at least a journeyman. Would she ever have time to become the master of seacraft she wished to be? She doubted it. But while it was her work, she would do it with all her might. One step at a time, she had told herself in those bleak days of utter discouragement. It was a good rule.

And now she looked at God's house built on this dot of an island on Jaluit Atoll. She did not guess how much her presence added to the delight of her parishioners. They had their own church, and today they had with them their own missionary who had come to them on their own ship. God was in his heaven and all was right with their world.

The lumber for their church had cost a thousand dollars and every cent of it had come from their own contributions, from the people of Jaluit Atoll! Not one dollar had come from the States. They were proud to be independent, to be self-sustaining. A thousand dollars! Eleanor turned this sum over in her mind. How much labor it represented in copra, dried in the sun, loaded in small boats and shipped finally to distant Japan! It was breath-taking, from the point of view of the meager economy of the islands. The people knew what they wanted and had given their substance for it. Eleanor felt that the seed of the gospel had indeed taken deep root in the Marshall Islands.

Five hundred people, fully one half the population of the entire atoll thronged about the church—everyone, indeed, who could get a canoe ride from his home island. There was an air of eager expectation. The center of interest was the front of the church. There a group of singers raised their voices in a new song, a song about a cross. As the song swelled, a man climbed the little steeple and set upon it a three-foot cross. From it four colored streamers whipped out into the wind. These streamers were marked N E W S. As Eleanor gazed up at them, Barton, the native pastor, said proudly, "Mother Wilson, do you know what those letters stand for?"

"Why, surely for the four directions," she answered.

He laughed a little self-consciously. "But they mean more than that. They spell out *News* and that cross says to the world that from this church the Good News of the Gospel is being carried to the four corners of the earth."

Then everyone who could, packed into the church. The overflow stood at the windows. This was the mother church of the atoll and everyone on Jaluit felt he had a part in it.

It was a most impressive dedication—the look of devotion on the faces of the people, their joy in their new church, their unshaken faith in the goodness of God, to which they had clung through the dark days of the war. It was something Eleanor locked away in her heart that she might keep it forever.

They could not linger at Imroij for they were due at Ebon, some hundred miles south, for Christmas. Ebon, or Boston Island, had been named by some early Massachusetts skipper and set down on his chart. It was the scene of the first arrival of the *Morning Star I* back in 1857. It is a beautiful and fruitful island, nearest of all the Marshalls to the equator, and quite different from the bleaker northern atolls. Three members of the *Star's* crew came from Ebon— Luckabudge, Lau, and Freddy. It is a sailor's dream to be home for Christmas. This year for them the dream would come true.

It was Christmas morning when the *Star* put in at Ebon, and let go her anchor in a safe spot where it would be possible for all the crew to go ashore. The Mother Church on Ebon was truly Marshallese. The prewar church had been demolished and the present thatched-roofed pavilion with open sides was of true native architecture. It was easy to imagine as one looked at it that it was still 1857. In such churches, the first missionaries preached the Word.

There was small need for closed sides to any building here except in rainy and windy weather. There were indeed compensations for this natural air conditioning. Not only did it give one-hundred per cent ventilation but there was an unobstructed view for all on the outside.

No one in the islands is lonely at Christmas, not if he can mingle with the island people. This is the great Community Day of the whole church year and everyone in every atoll takes part in it. Preparations begin the first week in November. Each community forms its own group and decides what its contribution will be—new carols, with their own words and often their own music, or a skit commemorating the coming of the first American naval vessel. For this last the singers were dressed in red, white, and blue, and standing in a pattern to represent the American flag. Still others acted out the story of Noah and the flood, with the waters of the Great Deluge poured realistically into a tub.

Eleanor watched and found her New England reserve breaking down, found herself feeling an integral part of this assemblage, all of them known to her, most of them her parishioners.

The singing was always wonderful. Who can sing like these island peoples? They have a natural sense of rhythm. The skits were excellent for the people are natural artists at pantomime. And best of all the whole program was a community matter. The idea of a solo was to them astonishing. No Marshallese ever thought of singing alone.

There were "Christmas tree" songs in a lighter vein, but a stranger might have looked puzzled, for there was no tree inside the church; nor did any decorations hang on the bent trunks or high clusters of leaves and nuts of the coconut trees outside. It would not be easy to decorate a coconut tree, unless a boy went aloft and gilded the great nuts where they hung. To the Marshallese, the "tree" was the corner where the presents were laid.

They take literally the injunction that it is more blessed to give than to receive. Each community pools its resources and there is some good-natured rivalry in the bringing of fine gifts. It is a white Christmas without snow. Everyone gives all he has. No one in the islands expects to have any money after Christmas. Naturally, he used what he had.

The gifts are piled in the "tree" corner—bags of rice, flour and sugar, luxuries of the islands, cases of soap and matches, dress lengths of cotton print cloth, three and a half or four yards long, men's cotton shirts and trousers—the things most needed for life in the islands.

But there is *no* Christmas dinner. No one has time to cook it or even to think of it. This is a feast of song! Each one has brought something to stave off hunger—a piece of breadfruit, a banana or the giant doughnuts made of unsweetened bread dough. Boys climbed trees and tossed down drinking nuts. Material wants were easily satisfied, and since Christmas dinner was a thing unknown, it was not missed. Christmas in the islands is a community day, not a home day; it is something in which everyone shares. Eleanor recalled a navy doctor on Majuro Island who was so touched by the true spirit of this day among the Marshallese that he exclaimed it had been the happiest Christmas he had ever spent in his life and he, a man, homesick for his wife and children back in the States. The devotion of these people, their songs of praise for the birth of the Christ child, the oneness of spirit were a revelation to a man whose love of Christmas had been somewhat dimmed by its commercialism in his own country.

Here, gifts were not exchanged. No one went away with booty. The gifts were carefully divided by a chosen committee among the pastor, the mission schools, the needy and the outside guests. These last would be given native fruits like the papaya and bananas. In good times even a live pig or chickens might be presented to special guests, and always island handicraft. This Christmas, Rong Rong Mission School received eighty dollars and a gift of food.

No one thought of going away that night. Perhaps there would be time to cook a little rice for supper. Then the sleeping mats would be spread. On Ebon each community has its own shelter house on the mission property. Eleanor slept at the home of Tokak, the local pastor. Everyone slept soundly even if the only bed was the hard floor. It had been a long day and much effort had been lavished on the entertainment. Rest was a necessity and sleep was golden. Had the notorious Captain Hayes, the pirate, attacked the island that night, not a soul would have wakened.

New Year's Day they arrived at Ailinglaplap. There was singing but little else. The first week in the new year is a week of prayer with daily prayer meetings. New Year's day is not a riotous time in the islands.

From Ailinglaplap, the *Star* went northwest to Kwajalein. Something new had been added to the mission program. Perez, the young navigator who had taught Eleanor to plot a course, invited them to put on a "show" for the enlisted men at the Acey-Deucey Club. The students from Rong Rong Mission were as delighted as if they had been asked to perform before the Queen at Buckingham Palace. The American servicemen were a most appreciative audience. They listened with the keenest interest. Few of them had had any real contact with the Marshallese, for even the civilian workers did not live here on the "Rock" where the navy post was located. Now they would have something with which to enliven their letters home.

The Rong Rong boys sang an anthem, *Wake the Song*, and the Negro spiritual, *I Ain't Goin' to Study War No' More*.

This last brought appreciative applauding from the young seamen and airmen.

Then, by request, the boys sang in Marshallese, first their school song and then a mission song composed by their own music teacher, Elanjo.

"Say," one navy boy ejaculated, "this is terrific! We should have held this at the outdoor movie so more of the boys could hear it. How these folks can sing!"

Then Eleanor gave a talk on the humorous side of native

customs and showed the men the drum and spear that had been used at the pageant on Rongelap. The young seamen roared as they learned that at a Marshallese wedding the presents were presented to the pastor who performed the ceremony. There were groans when they learned of a Christmas day celebration in which there was no Christmas dinner.

Then a group of girls from Ebeye across the water sang a group of stunt songs, with the hand clapping and gestures which every Marshallese girl learns. Its rigmarole language had no meaning that could be translated. It fell into a class with peas porridge hot, peas porridge cold. More Marshallese songs concluded the program. Then "cokes" were served, and a boy passed his navy cap and Rong Rong Mission School received a gift of fifty dollars. Eleanor felt that somehow that evening had made both singers and audience richer for a new experience.

Then it was time to go back to school at Rong Rong, with the octet of singers feeling like professionals back from a world tour.

In January, 1951, the *Star* lay at her anchor but February saw her heading for Mille, the southernmost island of the Sunrise Chain. It was some sixty miles from Majuro, and with the prevailing winds from the northeast, this was an easy run. They left before sunset so that they might get through the Pass by daylight, and arrive at Mille next morning.

Eleanor looked at the shore of Mille with keen interest. She had never been here on this far southern atoll, but she knew the Queen, Lanjin, plump as a Polynesian, a thing rather rare in the Marshalls. The Queen and two deacons of the church came out to greet her and stayed for lunch aboard the *Star*. Then she went ashore to visit the church. That Sunday she conducted all the Sunday services, baptized two babies and acted as family councilor. This time the problem was that of a divorced man who wished to remarry and still remain a church member. All Eleanor could do was remind him of the Marshallese Church rule which stated that a divorced person, whose mate was living, could not remarry and remain a communicant. He could contract a civil marriage, and if after ten years both parties had been faithful in church attendance and had brought their children to Sunday School and had the sanction of their local pastor, both he and his wife could then be reinstated to full membership.

Eleanor stayed with the Queen in what she supposed to be the Queen's house. She was astonished to learn that the Queen had "borrowed" the house for this visit because, she explained modestly, her house was not good enough. Eleanor was saying good-bye to the Queen and her little granddaughter, and the child was proudly exhibiting her pet turtle to the visitor. The Queen said, "You want to give your turtle to Mother Wilson, don't you?"

It was doubtful who felt the greater consternation at this bolt from the blue, the unwilling child or the reluctant missionary. Turtles were rather rare on Mille and the child had watched this one hatch from an egg. She had faithfully fed it and cared for it. To please the child, Eleanor had shown great interest in it, and it was this that had brought about this dilemma. What could she do? If she accepted it, the child was deprived of her pet; but if she refused it the Queen would have been deeply hurt, even insulted at the refusal of a gift. There was nothing to do but accept graciously. So the turtle in a bucket of water had a free ride aboard the *Star* to Rong Rong School.

One day in late February Luckabudge studied the sky with his seaman's "weather eye" look. "Mother Wilson," he said, "you know next month is not good for sailing. No one can tell what March winds will do. I hope you will not plan to take the *Star* outside the lagoon."

She understood. "I know that is wise, Luckabudge," she agreed. "We will postpone any trips until April."

So for a few weeks Majuro Atoll with its oval reef must be the edge of their horizon. Their only trips were down the lagoon inside the protecting wall of coral to islands that dotted the reef.

Easter they spent at Uliga at the other end of the atoll. Before strangers came to the atoll it was not the place of importance it is today. Majuro Island is the population center. But with Uliga the administrative head of the islands under the Navy, a great number of people were living there. Easter Sunday was Communion Day. Once the people would all have tried to reach the mother church on Majuro. But with so many working here at Uliga, that was not practical, nor did they have time enough to make such a journey, even if transportation could be found. The old navy chapel down by the sea could accommodate about three hundred, and many more could sit at the side and still be a part of the service.

There were special Easter songs sung by different groups. These came after the service and were not part of it. The idea of a choir was essentially strange to a Marshallese. It was true they would rehearse faithfully for two or three weeks for a special occasion but they had not been trained to the discipline of weekly choir practice. Luckily they were unused to accompaniment for there was no piano in the chapel, not so much as a tuning fork.

Whatever they lacked in training, they more than made up for in enthusiasm and native sense of rhythm. Everyone who has ever lived in the islands, will remember the harmonious singing of the Marshallese. Eleanor was sure that in years to come when she was back home for good, she could shut her eyes and recall the sights and sounds of "her islands" among which she was so thoroughly at home.

CHAPTER XIV

Off for Ponape

THE BIG EVENT after Easter on Eleanor's calendar was the May meeting of the American Board and the German Lieben-zeller Missionaries at Ponape in the eastern Caroline Islands. But how was she to get there? It was a very special meeting. Not only would Admiral Miller, navy chaplain, be there but also Edward Hayes, a representative of the Community Churches of the United States, and with him would come a delegate from "Brimstone Corner," the famous and historic old Park Street Church in Boston. She simply must attend. A way must be found! The plane fare was $92 round trip, even at the half-fare price charged to missionaries and other church workers. There was no $92 in her travel budget. And she could not "mount up on wings of eagles."

But there was money in the budget to run the *Morning Star!* Would she dare risk the eight-hundred-mile trip across open ocean? She could "island hop" to Kwajalein, then sail due west to Lae and Ujae, due south of Bikini, but separated from this forbidden atoll by a hundred and eighty miles of sea. From Ujae, Ponape lay southwest by west a distance of a little more than four hundred miles. Dare she attempt this voyage? She considered her problem carefully.

The *Star* was seaworthy. At least, her hull was sound! Her masts, sails, and rigging were still good, even though somewhat weakened by use in the months past. She had a good island crew and they worked with her, within reasonable limitations, as a team. They had begun to believe a little in the sextant but still clung stubbornly to steering by wind and wave and did not always tell her when they altered course. To them it was a matter of small consequence. They merely humored her, taking little stock in her chart and the method of dead reckoning.

The engine had failed them completely. But Eleanor had something else to count on now—fourteen months of bitter experience into which she had crammed enough sea lore to make a yachtsman envious. She knew from personal experience what seas could pound the *Star* without sending her to the bottom. She had hung off reefs in the long dark hours of the night and seen her crew kedge them off by dropping anchors from the dinghy, each time farther from the dangerous ledge and so gradually pull the schooner to safety. She knew how to live on short rations of water, and to eat cold and tasteless food. She felt sure of her navigation. While sun or stars shone she could get their position and put it on the chart. Only for set and drift of the current she could not allow accurately, for these shifted with the season, and the *Star* had to shift course a dozen times in a single night at the whim of the wind and the discretion of the island helmsman.

Ponape lay close to seven degrees north latitude. Even an old-time whaling captain could have found it by latitude sailing. Nature had provided "a pillar of cloud by day" in the sun; and "a pillar of fire by night" in the North Star. All one had to do was to strike the seventh parallel of latitude and keep on it by meridian, or noon shots, of the sun; and by observations of Polaris at night, always providing the Pole Star was not obscured by the usual great banks of cumulus clouds on the horizon. It took an experienced navigator to snatch a Polaris shot in the rare moments when the clouds parted to let the star shine through. But with any kind of luck he should sight the high island at a distance of twenty-five miles and sail straight into the Mant Passage in the reef. If by bad luck he missed this pass and was swept past the island, his lookout would surely sight the great Rock of

Jokaj, a straight cliff towering out of the sea at the north-west corner of this island group. It had been a whaler's land-mark time out of mind. Eleanor was sure she could make Ponape. Even if her watch failed and her sights were not perfect, their compass course was an easy one. The only hitch lay in the variable winds and currents.

It was hazardous but it was not foolhardy. Eleanor prayed long and earnestly and had the serene inward conviction that they were to go. Inside her, a persistent little voice kept whispering that Kusaie lay only a little off the route home, *if* she returned by the southern way, past Mokil and Pinge-lap. Kusaie! The very thought of going there thrilled her. It was her first home in all of Micronesia. She had so many friends there whom she longed to see before she went back to the States on leave. And good King John and his Queen Hattie were not growing any younger. It might be, if she did not see them now, that she would not see them on this earth again. One never knew what the future held. Some emergency might arise that would prevent another visit. But she could go now—*if* she could sail the *Star*. She listened to that voice, not certain whether it was the prompting of con-science or only the keen desire of her own heart. She made up her mind. Come what may, she was going to Ponape on her own ship and she was going to stop at Kusaie on the way back. The decision once made, she never thought of altering it.

She announced her decision next morning to her crew. "We will sail for Ponape by way of Kwajalein and return by Kusaie," she said, as if it were a routine voyage that no one would question. But immediately difficulties began to pile up in the path of the skipper of the *Morning Star*. Mejjon, the island captain, and his crewmen exchanged dubious glances. Mejjon shook his head. He had never been to Ponape. He was a Marshallese and Ponape was in the Caro-lines beyond the waters that he knew.

"Better take Lelet in my place," he said with finality. "He

sailed there on the *Star* with Dr. Hanlin. He knows the harbors of Ponape and Kusaie."

Eleanor felt this would be wise, for the currents made it tricky business entering Kusaie in particular. It would be wise to have an island captain who had been there before. She resolved to ask Lelet to take Mejjon's place. She was reasonably sure he could get leave of absence from his pastorate and would be glad to go. A trip to Ponape, a land of high mountains, was a treat to any Marshallese, used as they were to low atolls; and sailing a ship was a welcome diversion from the work of pastor and schoolmaster.

Then there was the matter of provisioning the ship. Somehow unless she did this herself, it was never done properly. She had no executive officer. As always, it was a one-man or a one-woman job. Her crew could sail! But they could not qualify as quartermasters. There was firewood to be got aboard before leaving Majuro. They could take on extra water and supplies at Kwajalein for any emergency. One never knew when a sailing ship might be becalmed.

When they reached Kwajalein she learned that they were out of matches, and so was the Island Trading Company and the Navy Stores! A Navy wife gave her two paper books of matches when she heard of her predicament. With these, they set out on a journey that might take many days. No one aboard owned so worldly a gadget as a cigarette lighter, and it never occurred to Eleanor to buy one!

She checked out with the Port Director and mentioned that she was first heading west from Kwajalein to Ujelang Atoll before going on to Ponape. The Port Director swung about in his chair.

"I do not advise that, Miss Wilson!" His tone was serious. "Do you realize how close you would be sailing to the restricted area about Eniwetok? Let me show you on the chart."

He jumped to his feet and, spreading out the chart of the northern Marshall Islands, he put his pencil point on Eniwetok just north of the tenth parallel of latitude. Ujelang was very close to the clearly marked out "Danger Area."

Eleanor thought for some minutes.

"It seems a shame to pass them by," she said regretfully. "You know how hard it must have been for these people to have left their own atoll of Eniwetok and be resettled there on Ujelang, and I have never heard of a complaint from one of them. I did want to visit them in their new homes and leave them a supply of new Bibles. I think it would make them feel closer to the other churches of the islands."

The Port Director nodded. He, too, felt keenly for these people whose home atoll had been taken over for atomic research, probably in perpetuity. Life for them at best had been meager. Many of the more northerly atolls of the Marshalls were relatively unproductive, some being uninhabited altogether. The poor soil and meager rainfall on many made it difficult or impossible to grow breadfruit; coconuts alone were the staff of life. True, plans were afoot to send a government agricultural expert to Ujelang to study their prob lem and to introduce varieties of food plants that might do well there. Until then, their diet would be largely coconuts and fish, the ancient staple foods of the islands, supplemented by such flour, rice and sugar as they could obtain in exchange for their copra.

Yet as Eleanor studied the chart she knew the Port Director was right. If they had any bad luck at all with southerly winds, they might be blown into the danger area.

"I will give up the plan to stop at Ujelang," she said. "Without an engine, I can see it is too great a risk."

The Port Director could not know what a blow this was to her. It meant she might not have another chance to visit these isolated parishioners for whose welfare and comfort she was particularly concerned.

It was while they were filling their water tanks from a Navy "mother ship" that a sailor cast a weather eye over the *Morning Star*.

"Where you bound, ma'am?" he asked.

"Ponape," she answered.

"Who's your navigator?" he asked curiously.

Eleanor pointed to herself.

"Wow!" he exclaimed in amazement, little short of horror. "Glad I'm not aboard!"

Once this would have nonplussed the lady skipper, but now she only laughed. They would reach Ponape! The only question was when.

On the afternoon of May 8, 1951, they set out on their Odyssey. The familiar lines came to her:

> I cannot rest from travel; I will drink
> Life to the lees. All times I have enjoy'd
> Greatly, have suffered greatly, both with those
> That loved me, and alone; on shore, and when
> Thro' scudding drifts the rainy Hyades
> Vext the dim sea.
>
> I am a part of all that I have met;
> Yet all experience is an arch, wherethro'
> Gleams the untravell'd world whose margin fades
> For ever and for ever when I move.
>
> 'Tis not too late to seek a newer world.
> Push off, and sitting well in order smite
> The sounding furrows; for my purpose holds
> To sail beyond the sunset, and the baths
> Of all the western stars, until I die.

But it was not so easy with this wind to sail beyond the western stars, and the margin of Kwajalein was not fading as rapidly as Eleanor could wish. They were out of South Pass and their course for Ponape lay west by south, two hundred and fifty-nine degrees true. But the wind was most uncooperative. Ulysses would have thought the gods frowned upon his journey. It was not much of a wind. Aeolus would have scorned to put it in his bag. And it was blowing from the southwest. The best they could do was to tack to the northwest and make as much departure or difference in longitude as they could. Their goal lay westward. Sailing

south was undesirable for fear of being caught in the dol-
drums and being becalmed. This was the dread of all sailing masters whether aboard the *Morning Star* or the ships
that bore the Greeks to Troy. And she had no rowers to
"smite the sounding furrows." If the wind died, they were
helpless.

Two days out they sighted Lae to the south of them. Lae
is the smallest inhabited atoll in the Marshalls. Between it
and Eniwetok lay only Wotho Atoll. Off Lae even the southwest wind failed them and they were all but becalmed. Lae
was less than a hundred miles from South Pass and they were
farther north than they wished to be. As darkness settled,
the sky clouded over. There was no use for the sextant, no
need to study wave patterns. There was not enough wind to
fill the *Star's* sails, nor was the current strong, but its set
was to the north.

Soon after dark they heard the roar of a plane. It was
a wonderfully comforting, homelike sound to one who had
lived near naval bases. Somehow they did not seem so alone
on the sea when the great sky bird passed overhead. Luckabudge waved a lantern to let the pilot know they had seen
him. But what was the matter with that plane? It was circling about them, and a small flare landed on the water not
a hundred yards from the *Star's* prow. The plane circled
again and dropped another flare, this time nearer to them.
This one seemed to be drawn as if by a magnet straight
toward the boat. Lelet was thunderstruck, uncertain what to
do. The crew stood gaping. It was Eleanor who thought she
understood the signals.

"Lelet, I fear we are getting into the danger zone about
Eniwetok! Those flares are a warning! We must have been
driven too close to the danger area by the currents. Make
south, if you can!"

Lelet shook his head and looked up, puzzled at the circling plane. This was all very well for the man up there,
with his great roaring motors and silver wings, to warn them

off. They were only poor seamen on a sailing ship almost without steerage way. He shook his head.

"Mother Wilson, how can I? We have not enough wind!"

The fourth day out they sighted Ujae. They were to the north of it, nearer to Eniwetok than they had been before. In seventy-two hours they had made only one hundred and fifty miles. At that rate, they would need all the food and water taken aboard for fear of calms. This day they managed to work a little to the southwest of Ujae, but they were never out of sight of the island. That night the wind shifted to the northeast, exactly where it would serve them best. It freshened steadily until they were making five knots on a direct course for Ponape. On the fourth day from Ujae, Lelet raised the cry, "Land-o!" Straight ahead of them mountains were rising out of the sea. That meant they had only twenty-five miles to go.

Ram, a newly enlisted sailor from Wotje in the Marshalls, whose whole world until now had been bounded by low coral atolls, stared transfixed at this vast mass toward which they were sailing. He sat at the forepeak as if unable to move or speak. Freddy and Luckabudge were "experienced" travelers. They had been to Kusaie, Ponape, and Truk. The others had all seen at least one high island. But Ram, for the first time "lifted up his eyes unto the hills."

They were off Mant Pass that night but dared not attempt to enter it in the darkness. They lay off the pass with just enough sail set to give them way, waiting for day. Two men were on watch as usual, and the watch was changed every four hours. Yet below in her cabin Eleanor was restless. About two in the morning something drove her on deck. She saw no sign of life. As she looked more closely, she saw a figure stretched out on the cockpit seat sound asleep. The helmsman! And where was the man supposed to be on watch with him to make sure he stayed awake? She went swiftly to the helm. It was lashed! And they were drifting only a few yards off the reef!

She did not waken the seaman. She sat down in the helmsman's seat and loosened the helm. There in the darkness she
kept watch. If the *Star* moved toward that reef, she could
rouse the sleeping seaman in the manner of an old-time
first mate! But miraculously the current seemed friendly to
them. The *Star* drifted parallel to the reef, never approaching any nearer to it. All she needed to do was guide the ship,
keeping her nose just a little to seaward. Just before the
watch changed at four in the morning, the man on the seat
stirred, then sat bolt upright. He stared at the lady at the
helm. He leaped up.

"Mother Wilson!" he cried in dismay. "I will take the
wheel." He could say nothing more. In all the Pacific islands
there was no more chagrined seaman than this man who had
been caught sleeping on watch.

"Oh, no," Eleanor said. "I am toban until daybreak."
"Toban" meant the man on watch. Since he had proved un-
trustworthy, there was nothing he could say.

Then Luckabudge appeared for his watch. He insisted
upon taking the wheel, but still she refused. It was not long
until daylight, and at the moment she was loath to trust
anyone but herself. The negligent sailor and his still more
negligent partner who was sound asleep in his bunk would
never live this down among their fellow crewmen, not so
much that they might have endangered the ship as that they
had been caught asleep on watch, and by a woman!

Only when they were safely anchored did Eleanor read
the crew a lecture on the dangers of lashing the helm at
night, for, should the helmsman fall asleep and the wind
change, the ship and all their lives might be lost.

It was only when she stepped ashore on Ponape that it
came to her almost with a sense of shock that they had made
a pin-point landing, having navigated mainly by compass
and with relatively no change of course since leaving Ujae.

The meetings were not at Kolonia where the *Star* landed
but Eleanor was met at the pier by Galleo, a faithful old

pastor. He had secured a skiff with an outboard motor to take her to the meetings at Owa about five miles away. The meeting did not require a hall for there were only six American Board Missionaries in the eastern Carolines and the Marshalls combined. The Reverend and Mrs. Terpstra of the Owa Mission on Ponape, Lela Morgan, a teacher in the Kolonia Church School, Anna Dederer and Mr. Kaercher of Truk; these with herself made up the complete staff of the Mission Board in the islands. With Admiral Miller and his two guests, the whole party numbered nine. The delegate from Park Street Church was Sigrid Helmer, an old friend of Eleanor's. Only Edward Hayes was a stranger. He had come out to investigate the Mission work in the islands with the idea of his church contributing toward it.

When the skiff touched at the shore below the house and Eleanor walked calmly into the meeting, Margery Terpstra rushed forward to greet her. The relief on her face was more eloquent than any words.

"Eleanor Wilson!" she exclaimed, embracing her. "Are we glad to see you! We have been looking for you these three days past!"

She did not say what they feared might have happened.

Then Anna Dederer's high-pitched voice broke in, "You know it was decided at the meeting on Truk a year ago that you were not to take the *Star* out of the Marshalls and preferably not out of Majuro Atoll!"

Eleanor smiled at her old colleague.

"Well," she said, "I had no money for plane fare. Did you think I could swim?" From this hour the legend of Eleanor as a skipper began to grow in size like a snowball rolling downhill. She could have told them it had been less dangerous and infinitely less nerve-wracking than the sixty-mile trip with her students to Aur.

She was thankful that two days of meetings remained in which she could discuss with her co-workers her mission business, make her report and submit her budget. Somehow problems shared lost their grimmer aspects. The Snows and the Sturgeses had faced the same problems here in the mid-nineteenth century: How to make the most of what resources they had, in personnel and in funds. The need for another American Missionary family in Truk and Kusaie was discussed; the curriculum for mission and Sunday Schools was planned, together with the thousand and one details of work in the Mission field.

But there was in the room something that seldom happened in a purely secular gathering. Here was a family united, who had met to draw strength for the work ahead. From this room they would go out with renewed courage to face the problems that lay before them in their parish of Micronesia. From these meetings Eleanor always drew strength for her work in her own parish which was essentially a lonely one.

CHAPTER XV

Kusaie—Pearl of the Pacific

It was the twenty-first of May before Eleanor was ready to set sail for home. She told no one of her intended route. Yet nothing in the islands can be done in secret, particularly making preparations for a voyage. By bird messenger, by bush telegraph, on the swift wings of rumor, word spread about Ponape that the *Morning Star* would return to the Marshalls by way of Kusaie.

As if Aladdin had rubbed his lamp, figures began to appear—men, women and children, all with their sleeping mats and food for a journey. They looked at Eleanor with complete trust. Inwardly, she groaned. Did she not have enough problems skippering her battered schooner about the tropic seas without the added responsibility of passengers?

"Where do you wish to go?" she asked, as calmly as she could.

"To Mokil!" Eight voices answered.

"To Pingelap!" This came in a single voice.

Nine passengers! It was true these islands lay directly or almost directly on her course to Kusaie, but neither had a sheltering lagoon where the *Star* might put in. She could only lie offshore and wait for outrigger canoes or Mokil whaleboats to come and take off the passengers.

"I can offer you only deck space," Eleanor warned them. "What will you do if we encounter rain or storm?"

They smiled broadly, these would-be travelers. What did

they care *where* they slept? For weeks they had been trying
to get passage to their home atolls. Here was their chance!
"We shall not mind rain," they said. "We are not afraid of
getting wet."

But Eleanor knew well enough what they would do! They
would crowd into the main cabin and take all the bunks,
leaving her crewmen to sleep where they might.

"And what about food?" she queried. "I simply do not
have food enough aboard the *Star* to feed nine extra people."

"We have our own," one woman said, patting a basket
of fruit and coconuts.

Yet Eleanor knew well that the meager supplies of the
Star's lockers would have to be shared among all these extra
mouths. But this was the mission ship and it was meant to
serve the island people. They would manage somehow. They
always had.

As if in answer to her dilemma, food began to arrive, food
for the journey and as gifts from the Ponapeans to islanders
who lived on low sandy atolls where there were no forests
to provide the luxuries of life. Onto the deck of the *Star*
went great stalks of bananas and other fruits, donors often
unknown. But where could they carry water for such a company even if they had containers for it? It would mean close
rationing all the way, a thing difficult for people who took
no thought for the morrow.

At last all supplies were aboard. Every available water jar
was securely lashed and covered. The passengers squatting
on the deck tried to make themselves small, but even so it
was difficult for the crewmen to get about. They were forced
to walk over the high piles of banana stalks! Eleanor thought
as they cast off, that the *Star* must look like a pirate ship,
loaded for a year's cruise, and carrying away captives. Only
there was no Jolly Roger at their masthead. Instead, their
craft carried the mission banner—the blue pennant with its
white dove!

Their course lay a little south of east. It was ninety miles to Mokil and seventy more to Pingelap. These islands were steppingstones on the three-hundred-mile journey to Kusaie, but they were small islands to find in a vast stretch of sea with southerly currents running strong. They had no more than started when the sea roughened and the rains began. Just as Eleanor had feared, all nine passengers crowded into the main cabin and preempted the crewmen's bunks. Eleanor tried hard to persuade the women to come back into her cabin but her words had not the slightest effect on them. The motion of the ship was noticeably worse aft, and the American idea of separate sleeping quarters for men and women was foreign to them. In the shelter houses about the church of each village men and women spread their sleeping mats. To them it involved no immodesty, no impropriety.

Here, perforce, Eleanor held evening prayers. Out came the copies of the famous Marshallese diglot scriptures—the New Testament and the Psalms—printed in parallel columns, one English, one Marshallese. The Mokil people looked hungrily at these books. They had no such Bible as yet in Ponapean, the language of which their own dialect was a variant.

"Won't you give us your Bibles?" they asked the crewmen. "You can get others in the Marshalls! We have none!"

And with typical island generosity, three of the *Star's* crew gave away these precious books to strangers they would never see again. These Bibles would be put to good use, in spite of the language handicap. There were people in Mokil and Pingelap who had worked in the Marshalls for the Navy and had learned Marshallese. And there were Marshall Islanders married to people on both atolls.

As expected, the winds were contrary, for the prevailing winds are from the east. The first night out they made so little progress that when morning came, the high mountains of Ponape were still in view off their stern. It needed no unusual sea sense to tell the lady skipper that they were in for a difficult passage. What manner of men had the early

Polynesian voyagers been, she wondered, that they could beat into the wind with their matting sails and keep on to the east? She thought of them many times in the days that followed.

These winds would slow them down, and the trip might last longer than she had anticipated. Bukmeto could be trusted to dole out their meager supplies of rice, beans and tinned meat but she would have to keep a sharp eye on the water casks. Three days of rough seas and sullen gray skies did little for the spirits of the company. The crew made no complaint at the loss of their bunks and their privacy. But they could not get their proper rest when off watch, sleeping in any chance corner that might temporarily be vacant. There was no singing and little chatter in the main cabin. Indeed, about the ship there was a kind of hush, as if life had been suspended and they were waiting for it to begin again.

Eleanor marked on her chart every change of course. But with the constant tacking back and forth, it was all but impossible to do this accurately. It was critically necessary to keep their dead reckoning position as there was no way of knowing when either sun or stars would be seen.

On the third night out the sharp-eyed islanders spotted Mokil. Eleanor could see nothing on the murky edge of the horizon. They could not expect small boats to come out to them over the reef in the darkness. They would have to wait till morning, hoping not to lose their landfall. All night long they beat back and forth, hovering off the reef. In the morning they were close in and the atoll was in plain view. And they had been seen! The famous Mokil whaleboats were being launched and several outrigger canoes were being run into the water. At first break of daylight everyone on this side of the island had seen the *Star* and guessed her errand. Soon they would be alongside to take aboard the passengers.

These boats had to be handled by masters for here there is no break in the coral and they must go over the reef itself.

No one who had ever seen the Mokilese cross their reef would forget it! The islanders leaped out and, waiting for the crest of a wave, shot their craft over the coral and leaped into it again. Sure-footed and seawise, they made easy work of it. They reminded Eleanor of the swooping, darting sea gulls who cared not a whit if the water closed for a moment over their heads.

There was more space now with the Mokil passengers ashore. The crewmen could go back to their bunks and there was room to move about on deck. And one more day should bring them to Pingelap. But even on the second day out they did not catch sight of it. Lelet wore a worried frown and Luckabudge studied the clouds. Had they missed it by not bothering to consult the compass when the skipper was safely asleep below?

At noon the sun broke through and Eleanor got a noon sight. A noon sight determines latitude only. This showed them eight miles south of the island but whether to the west or east of it, there was no way of knowing.

"Lelet," Eleanor said earnestly, "if you want to steer by waves, now is your chance! I don't know when the stars will come out to let me get a position we can trust."

But apparently today the waves told Lelet nothing. That night Eleanor watched, sextant in hand, hoping to glimpse a star but not one showed through. About midnight on the twenty-seventh they saw something that startled them. It was a light moving on the water. That meant another ship! In all her voyaging on the *Star,* only this and one other vessel ever crossed their path. But in the morning the sea was empty. Where had that craft gone and what had it been? They felt more lonely than ever—just one tiny speck of flotsam on the face of the deep. Then about five o'clock in the afternoon they sighted a small boat. This was no United States naval craft. What was it? It must be seventy-five feet long, and smoke was coming out of its exhaust pipe. A power boat! Then it must be Japanese, for no island fishermen or trader had a power boat of such size.

"Perhaps they can give us our position!" Eleanor exclaimed.

Luckabudge looked closely at the ship. He had sailed on Japanese ships in the days of the Japanese occupation.

"It is an Okinawan boat," he said positively.

They sailed close up to the craft and Eleanor called to the boatmen in Japanese. Most Okinawans speak the language of their ancient conquerors. They themselves were of mixed Chinese and Japanese ancestry.

"Kon nichiwa, Osoreirimus ga watakushi tachi wa doko desu ka?" she shouted through her cupped hands. All of this meant, "Good day! Excuse me, but where are we?"

The Okinawan boatman stared at them, impassive as a Chinese idol. Six or seven crewmen joined him and lined the rail. They stared dumbly, apparently unable to speak. The sight of a woman—and a white woman at that—crying out to them in what was undoubtedly Japanese, was simply too much for them. If they had seen a ghost, they could not have been more astonished.

Eleanor tried again. "How do you do?" she called. "Can you give us our latitude and longitude?"

They chattered among themselves like excited children but gave no answer to those aboard the *Star*.

Then Luckabudge tried his Japanese. Not as correct as Eleanor's, his might more nearly approximate the dialect of Okinawan fishermen.

"Where is Kusaie?" Luckabudge shouted.

At last the boatman understood. He darted into the wheelhouse and came out again.

"Kusaie—North—East!"

"North!" Eleanor and Luckabudge exclaimed together. Then the currents had driven them far to the south! They must have missed Pingelap altogether. They called their thanks and swung as far to the north as the wind would permit. Eleanor waved. Delighted that they had been understood, the Okinawans waved back. In the camaraderie of the sea there is no barrier of race or nationality.

That night she got a star fix and certainly the Okinawans were right! Kusaie lay to the northeast. For the next two days they sailed northeast, but at a snail's pace, logging scarcely twenty miles a day. Then they had a west wind which enabled them to make better progress on their course. Yet when night fell they had not sighted Kusaie. It was just before daybreak next morning that they saw it, its cloud-topped mountains like something in a dream, something out of fantasy. How well that ragged outline of mountains was etched into Eleanor's memory. Kusaie, the Pearl of the Pacific, her first home in the islands. She had come to love it more than any spot on earth.

All that day they bore directly toward Kusaie but could not reach it. It was always there, beckoning to them. Nor when night came could they make out any lights, for the houses on Kusaie are for the most part not on the beach, but hidden behind a screen of trees. Eleanor ceased to worry about the compass course, for now the stars were out and by them her mariners could keep on course. It seemed they did this by instinct, not by conscious observation. They did this so well that when daylight came, the *Star* was nearing the harbor of Lelu.

Kusaie was old in missionary history. It was here to this high island, then called Strong's Island, that the first American missionaries to Micronesia had come in 1852. With them were Hawaiian converts. They had come bearing no weapons to defend their lives except the Word of God, their own courage, and a rather amazing letter from King Kamehameha III of Hawaii.

Eleanor had often wondered how they had made its contents known for it had been written in English. Had the Kusaiens learned enough English from the whalers to grasp the meaning of this astonishing message? Surely no Kusaien spoke Hawaiian so he could converse with the Polynesians. Even the legend of the Land of the Fiery Mountain, so far off to the northeast, must have grown faint with the centuries, if indeed it had ever been current here on Kusaie.

Yet the King seemed to have no difficulty in understanding the mission of the newcomers. Eleanor had tried many times to picture the scene—the King of Kusaie, doubtless suspicious of the white-faced strangers, if not of their Hawaiian friends; the half-savage islanders; and the few sullen renegade white men on Kusaie, hostile to any influence but their own in this island.

The message from Kamehameha read:

". . . I therefore take the liberty to commend these good teachers to your care and friendship, to exhort you to listen to their instructions. . . . I have seen the value of such teachers. We, here in my islands, once lived in ignorance and idolatry. We were given to war, and we were very poor. Now my people are enlightened. We live in peace and some have acquired property. Our condition is very greatly improved . . . and the Word of God has been the great cause of our improvement. . . . I advise you to throw away your idols, take the Lord Jehovah for your God, worship and love Him, and He will bless you and save you. May He make these new teachers a great blessing to you and your people and withhold from you no good thing."

What manner of people had they been, these first missionaries, Dr. and Mrs. Snow at Kusaie, and Dr. and Mrs. Sturges at Ponape, and all the others! They must have been made of the stuff of martyrs blended with the hardihood of the first American pioneers. They had faced hunger, drunken crewmen and dissolute whites, and a native people steeped in heathenism, whose only contact with the white men had been with the whalers, who often forgot in the equatorial seas that they were Christians on the other side of the earth. Many times they faced death but they had stayed! And their work had grown until Kusaie was the stronghold of the Congregational Church in the Pacific.

It was early in the morning when the *Star* went through the pass into the harbor. As always, Eleanor's heart contracted with the wonder and the beauty of this scene. The sun was shining and the mountain peaks were mirrored on the water, ruffled only by a light breeze and by the canoes coming out to meet them. This was the port of Lelu, the port royal of the islands. King John would be waiting to greet them. Once he would have paddled out in his own canoe, built by himself, to convoy them in. But now he was too old.

Then she saw the king's son, Ernest, coming to meet them, as etiquette demanded. Eager voices called to her. She heard her name over and over, as more and more canoes swarmed about the *Star*. Her New England reticence was sorely tried. She fought back tears. She saw so many familiar faces. These were the reasons back of the long voyage, the many hardships, the very real risks. She had wanted desperately to see Kusaie again. Well, she was here! In a moment she was over the rail, into a canoe, and was being paddled rapidly ashore toward Pijin, the village where her own house stood. The path from the landing to her house was lined on either side by Kusaiens, eager to grasp her hand in welcome and at the very end of the line stood the aging King John. Only Queen Hattie, the Kasra, was nowhere to be seen.

The venerable old man spoke words of greeting in Kusaien. He was too deeply moved to attempt to express himself in an alien tongue. And to Eleanor's lips flooded the right words for answer, words half-forgotten in her long stay in the Marshalls.

"Mother Wilson," the King exclaimed. "You have come home! We knew you would. We were sure. But it has been so long!"

"Where is Kasra?" Eleanor asked anxiously, almost ignoring his words. It was not like her old friend, the Queen, to be absent on such an occasion.

"She is sick, too sick to come." The old King tried to keep anxiety out of his voice. "She is waiting for you at home. I shall return to her and you come as soon as you can."

"Very well, Togusra," Eleanor said.

Togusra means King in Kusaien.

The old man shook his head. "Do not call me Togusra," he said gently, "for I am no longer King. You must not forget that now we are a democracy. And I am something much better than a King! I am a Pastor!"

Eleanor smiled with deep understanding. She herself had ordained King John to the ministry. When he became a pastor, he reached the height of his ambition. But he was old, and a pastor on mountainous Kusaie must travel at times by canoe to the three other villages, besides serving in his own. He had to go in all sorts of weather and in a region where the annual rainfall is measured in feet, not in inches. Plainly this would be beyond an old man's strength, so at the same time, she had ordained a younger man to be his helper.

King John was a magnificent man, of great warmth of heart, strength of mind, and that mysterious force which the Polynesians call "mana," a kind of divine essence. Perhaps our nearest word for it is personality, or better, character. He had some source of inward strength that nothing external could alter.

Even the Japanese conquerors of the island became aware of this quality in the now deposed native king.

"I heard that a Japanese official treated you very harshly during the war," Eleanor said regretfully.

King John nodded gravely. "Yes, he did," he admitted, but then added brightly, "but I got even with him!"

Eleanor was astonished to hear the King say this for she had thought the saintly old man incapable of malice or of a desire for revenge.

"What did you do?" she asked curiously.

King John smiled. "When he was hungry, I sent him food!"

She might have known! King John was a doer as well as a hearer of the word! And it had worked, as the good man never doubted it would. The astonished Japanese officer had come to him and asked humbly about the religion the King practiced. So for the first time the King had an opportunity to tell him about his God! No wonder King John was more pleased to be a pastor than anything else in the world. He had found his true vocation.

She noted that her host carried his most prized possession, a beautiful Bible with his name on the cover in gilt letters: King John, Kusaie. This had been the gift of the Massachusetts Bible Society.

Even the King had only one name, surnames being originally unknown in the island. After the coming of Europeans and Americans the islanders used their father's name for a surname, if more than their given name was required for identity. Occasionally a title was added, thus the King was sometimes called John Sigra.

Eleanor watched the erect form of the old pastor as he walked out of the mission yard. What an example and inspiration he had been to his people, all of his long life! When he had gone, she turned to Palik, who had come down from the Mission School at Mwot to welcome her.

"I was deeply grieved to hear of the death of your father, Palik," she said gently. "We shall all miss Kefwas. He was so much a part of the mission life here on Kusaie, that I cannot imagine this island without him."

Palik nodded solemnly. He had reason to revere the memory of the man who had adopted him as a son.

"Yes, we miss him!" he said. "But we can be happy for him. He has gone to a better world for he died in the Lord."

Everyone in Kusaie knew the story of Kefwas. He was the son of a Negro whaleman from an American ship, which back in the 1840's had touched briefly at this island. His mother had been a Kusaien girl. He must at one time have had some family connections on the maternal side, but within the memory of living people he seemed to have had no relatives. Perhaps he was simply so old that all of them had died. He had never had any children of his own.

"How old do you suppose Kefwas really was?" Eleanor asked.

Palik shook his head. "Who can say? There is no one alive

who can remember when he was born. I have asked the oldest people on the island. They all say that when they were young Kefwas was already a grown man. There was always Kefwas, they say. It is as if they expected him to live forever."

"He must have been nearly a hundred!" Eleanor said. "Why, he could distinctly remember our first missionaries here, Dr. and Mrs. Snow. And he remembered when the *Morning Star I* came to Kusaie!"

They stood in silence recalling the striking old man who had been such a unique figure. No one could have mistaken Kefwas for a Solomon Islander. Plainly his background lay in Dixie. Even his voice was soft and well modulated, his manner gentle as if he had been trained in the great house with the white pillars. He was part of a tradition of which he knew nothing. Yet certainly he had inherited something from the father he had never seen.

He had felt an instinctive loyalty to the American missionaries. He must have lived in childhood near the mission for Dr. Pease, then the resident missionary, had taught him at an early age to read and write English, had instructed him in the Christian religion, and had left upon him the indelible mark of his own fine character. Kefwas spent his life as handyman and teacher at the school. He was able to help Miss Baldwin translate the Bible into Kusaien and, in his eighties, had acted as Eleanor's interpreter when she preached in his district of the island. Kusaie would never be quite the same place without this man who seemed to tie past and present together. She was sorry that he was buried at the distant village of Tafwensak; she would have liked to visit his grave.

One thing she felt she must do on this visit, however arduous the journey. She must visit the grave of Elizabeth Baldwin, whose life had been given to the work here. Who could tell when she would see Kusaie again? As she walked toward the king's house, Eleanor mused to herself. The king was old. The queen, too, was aging and was now in poor health. Probably this would be her farewell visit with them and with many of her Kusaien friends. When and if she came again, she could not expect to see all of them alive.

Eleanor found the queen sitting up on her sleeping mat to welcome her. They embraced and at first spoke no words. Queen Hattie, or Kasra, as she was called in the language of the island, was a Kusaien only by adoption. She was born on Nauru, a tiny island on the equator, and her father was an American. Beloved in the islands, she had given to her people love and devotion. She was a midwife and once, when called upon to deliver a child that was a breech presentation, she had explained her therapy. "First I prayed to the Lord, and then I washed my hands in Listerine." This was the only disinfectant on the island.

How much greater was the bond of the spirit than the bond of blood, Eleanor thought, as she broke bread with these old friends in this familiar house. They had prepared their best but if it had been only biru, it would have been a feast. Eleanor shut from her mind the thought of the time when she must retire and leave this land of sea and coral atoll forever. Or had she become so much a part of it that, like the Baldwins, she would go on living in her little prefabricated house at Pijin?

Eleanor recalled earlier days. When the king heard she was returning, in January 1947, he had his men in each of the four villages build one quarter of the house. These portions were carried to the site and lashed together so perfectly that no one would have guessed how the house had been built. Each wall had come complete with openings for windows and doors. Glass was unobtainable and unnecessary in this climate. Metal screening was available and was quite adequate. Here even a small pension would give her a comfortable living. That precious thing, her own house, would always be waiting for her. Would she ever again want to settle down to live in Cambridge, Massachusetts? Would the stark outline of oak and pine seem as strange to her as the swaying coconut palms had on that long ago evening—

her first on Kusaie, when the village band had played "Home Sweet Home?"

They talked a long time together, as old friends will after long separation. The King and Queen told her what life had been like here in the war years, when Japanese rule became anything but benign. Often they were hungry, and once, Queen Hattie said, actual famine threatened them. She and the women and girls prayed before they went out to fish. Oddly enough, it is the Kusaien women who do most of the fishing. Suddenly in the shallow waters beyond the harbor of Kusaie there appeared a multitude of strange black fish, good to eat and so easy to catch that small girls could go out with nets and bring them in. After the war, they were seen no more.

"We were fed by the hand of God," the Queen said to Eleanor.

Certainly it was a strange coincidence that these fish arrived just in time to save the people from hunger. Had the currents in the sea altered or the temperature of the water changed to drive some new species of fish into these equatorial waters? Could falling bombs have disturbed some ancient feeding ground, causing the fish to change their migration routes through the seas? There was no ichthyologist to solve the riddle. To the Kusaiens none was needed. In ancient days, sorcerers had prayed men to death when heathen gods ruled the islands. Was it strange to think that a good God should answer a devout prayer for life?

Now they told her all the news of the island, matters that would concern only their own close circle. So-and-so had died, such a girl had fine twins, such a boy was away at school in Truk. There was a new church built in such a village. So-and-so had, alas, fallen from grace but they hoped to win him back into the church.

She noted that in the yard of the king's house stood a partly finished canoe. The king was jack of all trades and master of not a few; he was never idle. Even as he sat with them after luncheon, he was rolling coconut husk fiber against his thigh with one skilled hand, twisting it into the stout sennit that was the only cordage of the islands. Without it no voyaging canoes could ever have made their incredible journeys, for it tightened when wet, lashing the outriggers of the canoes ever firmer to the supports.

Eleanor recalled the fine eighteen-foot canoe that the king had made for her and, before he would permit her to use it, he had personally tested it in rough water outside the reef. His gift of a house and a canoe had made her really independent, a precious thing for anyone coming to the island. It did not occur to her that this was a completely unique honor accorded only to beloved missionaries.

As soon as proper, Eleanor returned to her home that the king always kept in good repair. This house here at Pijin had had many visitors. At the memory of one of these Eleanor laughed outright. He was a young Navy man who back in 1948 had asked wistfully if he might come ashore and spend the evening with her. She knew the signs. This boy was homesick and she seemed a touch with home. When he took his leave, he asked with some diffidence if her boys could paddle him out to his ship, not to the gangway, but to the forward anchor chain. Then Eleanor understood. He had gone AWOL to spend the evening chatting with a gray-haired lady missionary! Well, her boys could paddle softly. She spoke to them in Kusaien. They nodded. Not a sound would betray the presence of their canoe to the officer of the watch.

Barton, a mission man, wanted to see the big ship. Foolishly the young Navy man agreed. How Barton was to get off again apparently occurred to neither of them. Barton went up the chain first, hand over hand with the ease of an islander who has climbed coconut trees all his life. The young American seaman was close behind. But a hand shot out and grasped the astonished Micronesian, and a sharp voice rang out in the night. The anchor watch was alert! It was too late to retreat. Barton was caught and there was nothing for the lad who was AWOL to do but keep on climbing to meet the same fate. Barton never got to see the engine room which had been his dream. He was ingloriously thrust down the gangway to be picked up by his startled comrades in the mission canoe. He carried the story back to Eleanor. What would that young man tell the officer of the watch? That he had been ashore visiting a lady missionary from Boston? She longed to write a letter of explanation, but decided against it. There was no knowing what the young man had said, and it would be worse for him if she gainsaid his excuse. She doubted he had told the truth, as it certainly would not have been believed. He probably had suffered no worse punishment than rating extra duty and a small black mark on his record.

Eleanor looked at the tall coconut palms on the mission property.

"We must have new coconuts planted, to have young trees in bearing," she thought. "These are growing old."

It was hard to imagine that these trees were not native to the islands but had been planted here by the firstcomers, many centuries ago. What a tropic paradise this island was. Pineapples grew almost without care. Breadfruit thrived, as well as all manner of tropical fruits.

Small wonder that many a whaler deserted his ship at this island, Eleanor thought. In the hard 1840's life at sea was a brutal one. The common man had no rights and discipline was enforced by kicks and blows. And so meager were wages back home that there was little to hold him there. Money income was small in the islands, but money was not needed. Most of a man's needs could be satisfied by merely stretching out his hand.

Eleanor often wondered if the islanders' way of living was not superior to that of the outlander. He worked when it pleased him, never under stress. He enjoyed what he did. He was not lazy, as so many strangers thought. He *was* a spasmodic worker. Yet in the end he supplied his wants and lived without tension. Much of this simplicity of life might be laid to the lavish gifts of the coconut tree. No other tree gave man such rich and varied gifts: food to eat, milk to drink, fuel for fire, light for his lamp, cordage for his canoes. Even a coarse bark cloth came from the base of its growing leaves. The lagoon swarmed with fish and the shore with crabs. It was a little Eden set down in the Pacific.

Kusaie is not really one island, but a little group of eight islands clustered within one coral reef. It is a world in itself. Here one does not feel shut in as on a low atoll surrounded by the sea. The landscape is varied, with high mountains, rich forests filled with tropical fruits, and rivers and waterfalls. The individual islands were separated by a network of narrow waterways. To go from one to the other, one had only to pole a canoe through the tangled mangrove swamps. Here the water was so shallow and so full of roots that paddles were all but useless. The largest island, Ualan, is eight miles long and three miles across. There are nearly fifty square miles of land in the Kusaien group—a large world to island people. And in it they could move about safely without large boats.

The people lived in villages set just above the shoreline. Coconut palms grew everywhere. Many people went up the mountain slopes to cultivate their other crops. As in Hawaii and other island groups, directions—east and west, north and south—had little significance. One went inland up the mountain or down the mountain toward the sea.

She heard singing down by the shore. She listened to the wind rustling the stiff fronds of the coconuts. She heard the numberless small voices of the familiar jungle. A sense of deep peace came over her. She was home, home in her own house, home on Kusaie.

Early next morning they set out, Eleanor and some of the Star's crew, to visit the mission school at Mwot. It was to Mwot that Eleanor had first come as a teacher, back in 1936. It lay some distance from the port of Lelu. Luckabudge and the other Marshallese were curious to see the wonders of swamp, river, forest and mountain. They took Kusaien boys to pole for the Marshallese might easily have upset them, unused as they were to shallow waterways. The knack lay simply in thrusting the pole in at an angle, never straight. The waterway led them through the mangrove swamp. It would broaden out, then narrow to a mere canoe's breadth through which they had almost to force their way. Eleanor smiled, remembering how a crew of Marshallese girls had once upset them, teacher, students and lunch baskets all getting a wetting in the stream.

"We will stop at the Herrman plantation to visit Miss Baldwin's grave," Eleanor told her boat boys.

They demurred a little.

"Mother Wilson, it is a long hard climb for you," they objected. "And the Herrman plantation is out of our way."

But Eleanor was adamant. She could make it even though it was a trail suited to a mountaineer. The Herrman plantation was a prosperous one. Mr. Herrman was the second generation of his family in the islands. He had come out from California to help his uncle with his plantation and trading boat. Now his nephew had come out to help him. Both had married Kusaien women and had become part of the life on Kusaie. Through all the years the Misses Baldwin had been at the mission, he had been their friend. Many good things from the shelves of his store found their way to the Baldwin table, and many services had been rendered them.

They poled in to the Herrman landing. There was the great shoot for loading coconuts. Nothing had changed, it seemed, except herself. Eleanor thought of this as she toiled up the steep trail that led to the little private cemetery plot. In 1936 she had climbed as agilely as her students. But this was 1951! She paused to rest once or twice but for very pride pushed quickly on. Soon she could see the great white stone through the thick growth of the jungle. The boys dropped back a little, with the instinctive feeling of respect for another's grief. Indeed, in many islands it was taboo to approach a grave unless one came of the same lineage as the dead.

Here was the double grave with the great granite headstone sent all the way from Japan. Only one grave was filled. Elizabeth Baldwin had died here, her sister Jane back home in the states. Yet, fittingly enough, both their names were on the headstone, only one with the dates. Jane had intended to be buried beside her sister. She said she would not last long after her sister had gone.

"We are like a pair of scissors," she exclaimed. "One blade is useless without the other."

Eleanor had taken Miss Jane home to America early in 1941 when war threatened. She was nearly blind and the thought of living through another war appalled her. The Japanese official on the island had assured them that war would not come.

"Japan will not start it, because she could not possibly win," he said with finality. "And America will not start it, for she has nothing to gain. But *if* it should come, I will personally make myself responsible for the welfare of you ladies at the mission."

Yet Eleanor was glad that she had gone home. Tales of internment under the Japanese were not pleasant to recall.

As she stood beside the grave, she marveled once more at the life and work of these two women who came of staunch Pilgrim stock. Their brother had been a missionary in Turkey. They were women of independent means and already in their forties before 1900, when they came out to teach first in Truk. In 1912, they came to Kusaie, to the famous old Mission Training School of the Congregational Church. It was characteristic of them that they asked the Mission Board to send them to a place where no one else wished to go!

Miss Elizabeth was the more strong-minded of the two sisters, the dominant personality. Miss Jane made no decisions without consulting her elder sister. The work they did was nothing short of phenomenal.

Elizabeth and Jane were wonderful examples of the dedicated life. For nearly thirty years they lived on Kusaie, never once leaving it, even on retirement. They rarely moved about, even among the villages inside the reef. Mwot, the mission school site, and the port of Lelu where they went for their mail were their world and upon it they left their indelible mark.

Officially they went out as schoolteachers, but their great work was translating the Bible into Kusaien, a staggering task. Time meant nothing to the two sisters. About once a month a Japanese steamer touched at Lelu, bringing them old magazines from home, which they read and reread from cover to cover. With some consternation these two staid ladies, born when good Queen Victoria set the fashions, regarded the pictures of the low-cut gowns in the American periodicals and promptly cut these out before allowing their students to read the magazines. The official dress of the school was the Mother Hubbard. It had taken some time for Eleanor to coax the girls in her gymnasium class to put on the middies and bloomers that were already out-of-date at home. Two girls absolutely refused to expose their legs in this unseemly fashion. To island eyes, this was the ultimate of feminine immodesty.

But for all this, no one who ever stopped at Mwot felt any desire to ridicule. Here the two valiant sisters lived in a self-sufficiency bred of courage, isolation and high purpose. The face of Miss Elizabeth, even when in her seventies, was arresting. She had gone blind in the Lord's work, but a light shone in her countenance. From the workroom under the house came the sound of a foot press. This was the print shop. But there was no room there for the finished pages of the Bible. These were stored in racks in the Baldwins' living room, leaving them barely space to move about. Elizabeth lived to see her work finished. The Bible, from Genesis to Revelation, was now available in the language of this island! And they had already translated and printed *Pilgrim's Progress* both in Kusaien and in Marshallese. This

was much easier to do than the Bible because of the beautiful simplicity of the story. John Bunyan in Paradise must
have felt a glow of pleasure. From debtor's prison, his
words had reached to these far islands of whose very exist-
ence he probably did not know.

As Eleanor stood beside Elizabeth's grave she thought of
the magnificent lines Stephen Vincent Benét had written in
John Brown's Body. Though they described the valiant Scottish ancestress of a proud southern family, they would have
provided an equally fitting epitaph for Elizabeth Baldwin,
spinster, of Kusaie.

> To die at last as she wished to die
> In a fief built out of her blood and bone
> With her heart for the Hall's foundation-stone.

Elspeth MacKay had her candlesticks; Elizabeth Baldwin,
her Kusaien Bible.

Eleanor lifted her heart in prayer, and turned back. The
boys were waiting well down the trail and for a little way
she descended alone through the thick jungle growth. Far
away a bird screamed, its peculiar call a familiar one to her
ears. There was a humming of insects in the hot still air. At
the shore, they embarked again for the rest of the journey
to the school. Strange that Miss Elizabeth was not buried
there where she had done her life's work!

In the canoe the young people had been talking and
laughing, the crewmen of the *Star* exclaiming over the wonders of the mangrove swamp. Suddenly silence fell, a silence full of meaning. They were coming to a canal built
back in German days to avoid a long and arduous portage.
Eleanor understood the change of mood. This was the fabled
residence of an ancient nature god of the island, one responsible for providing the islanders with food. Luckabudge, who had come along to visit his daughter then at the
Mission School, strained his ears with the others. As a Marshallese, this legend was not part of his particular heritage.
There was only dead silence. Apparently the god did not

speak nor show himself in the presence of an ordained Chris-
tion minister! Eleanor looked meaningly at the Kusaien
boys and said, smiling, "I guess there are no crabs scratching
on tin roofing today!"

The boys laughed. This was the sound that had once terrified the crew of Mr. Herrman's boat at this dread spot.

The approach to the school property looked natural.
There were the mangrove roots reaching above the surface
of the water, the canoe house on the old pier, and up on the
side of the mountain Eleanor caught sight of the old Baldwin residence where she herself had lived before the war.
The canoe had been spotted and down the mountain path
ran the students and teachers to welcome their visitors.

Again it was a climb fit only for a mountain goat. Years
in the low Marshalls made one lose his skill at mountaineer-
ing. At last they came to a clearing on the slope. The path
turned suddenly and they were looking at the compound
of the Mission School. The scene was one of partial desolation. Only the cement posts of the school building itself
remained. The wood of the mission buildings had been
taken by the Japanese to build shelter huts on the mountain,
far from a spot they felt would be bombed. Eleanor felt a
little stunned. She knew the school had been demolished,
but somehow she had not been quite prepared for this ruin.
In her mind's eye, she had always pictured it just as it had
been when she left Kusaie in 1941. The school had been
built here first when Spain ruled the islands. It was hard to
think it should not be rebuilt under American trusteeship.

But the Baldwins' house had outlasted the bombs. Was
there something indestructible about these women? Even a
war could not obliterate the marks of their residence here.
The house had been repaired, the bullet holes stopped up,
and it was still in use.

There was a new chapel on the grounds, beyond the site
of the former school building, and here Palik, the adopted
son of Kefwas, was holding school. He looked at Eleanor,

wondering what her reaction would be to the meager beginning they had made. She had only praise to offer.

"You have done very well to keep the school going with
your missionaries on furlough," she commented.

He modestly gave credit to Frank and Srue who had
helped him ever since the days of the Baldwin sisters; and to
Flora, a daughter of King John and Queen Hattie, who was
matron of girls as well as teacher at the school. Palik insisted
on showing them his garden farther up the "hill." Feeding
sixty students and their teachers had presented grave problems but now food was coming from the garden. And, of
course, there were always coconuts, and breadfruit and bananas in season, and there were fish caught in the lagoon.
The people of the four villages often came bringing food
for the students. The pineapple gardens were gone and
there was no tapioca but Palik maintained the school and
was keeping the students happy.

Eleanor climbed to the second floor of the chapel to see
where the girls slept. Sleeping mats on a clean floor were all
that was required. Flora shared their quarters. Mission girls
were chaperoned at all times. This was an infallible rule
since the days of the first missionaries. The boys slept in
their dilapidated dormitories part way down the mountain.

As she was talking with Palik, Luckabudge came by with
his daughter. She was overcome with joy at having her father
visit her. It was seldom, if ever, that a Marshallese student
had a parent come to see her in remote Kusaie.

Luckabudge looked about sadly at the ruins of the once
fine school. "Oh, Mother Wilson," he exclaimed, "it is too
bad! Your beautiful school—it is all destroyed!"

Eleanor shook her head. "Not *all* destroyed, Luckabudge.
It is heartbreaking to think that such a fine school was torn
down to build shelters against our own bombs. But it is
only the buildings that are gone. A school is more than a set
of buildings; it is made up of people. In every district in the
eastern Carolines and in all the atolls of the Marshalls there

are graduates of this school. And think of the thousand Bibles Miss Baldwin printed here that have gone all over Kusaie; and all the copies of *Pilgrim's Progress* that have brought inspiration to thousands of people on many islands. The school is not gone, really. Good work goes on forever."

Luckabudge had not thought of this. He nodded solemnly. Still, he was a practical man, and it was a good thing to see a school in solid reality as well as to think of it as a thing of spirit. They were, of course, "making school" in the chapel with what books they had but it was not the same thing. The famous old school buiding *was gone* and it was a sore loss. It had been solidly built of good American lumber and under the supervision of an American architect. It would take time, money and devotion to build another on those strong cement foundations.

When Eleanor left here with Miss Jane Baldwin in the spring of 1941, the school was left in charge of a Japanese teacher. Few people in the United States realized how many Japanese Christians there were, or how strong the Congregational Church was in the land so soon to be at war with the western world. This principal had an able assistant in a promising Marshallese teacher, Isaac Lanwi, who later became the famous oculist of the Trust Territory. The Japanese soldiers came to the school and destroyed the type of his printing press so he could not use it "to send messages." That was a tribute to the power of the printed word. Yet the occupation here on Kusaie had not been brutal as it had been on Truk, where the starving Japanese, by-passed by our armies and cut off from their own, first ate leaves and then some few, gone mad perhaps with hunger, were accused of turning cannibal and eating human flesh.

Isaac was a pure Marshallese, so was not suspected of Caucasian sympathies. Perhaps the Japanese did not know that his wife, Mary Heine, was one quarter Australian. Perhaps it was their isolation here at Mwot that saved them or, perhaps, Eleanor thought, the Lord had spared Isaac and Mary to do his work. It was students like these who brought to a

teacher or missionary her ultimate reward. Certainly the old
faith brought by the Snows in 1852 had endured on Kusaie.

As she crossed the compound, Eleanor smiled to see a
stick stuck in the ground to form a crude sundial. She recalled that when workmen were building the boys' dormi-
tory, they had done this same thing to keep track of time.
She had shown them how to draw a circle about it and to
divide it into twelve equal parts to mark off the hours. Their
blank faces showed that they did not understand. She
learned that there was no word for hour in Kusaien! The
very concept had no equivalent in their minds. The sun
was there, there, or there in the sky, they said, pointing to
the position the sun had occupied at the given time or when
a certain event took place. Unless one were setting out on
a journey, time mattered little to them. Tides were the important thing and these changed daily. It was this disparity
of concepts that made teaching in Kusaien or any other
island language so difficult.

Back at Pijin, Eleanor was astonished to see Nelson, another son of King John. He grinned at her a trifle sheepishly.

"Why, Nelson!" she exclaimed. "When did you come back
from the Puluwats?"

She herself had sent Nelson as teacher to this remote island west of Truk, and Truk lay beyond Ponape, nearly a
thousand miles from Kusaie.

"I told my father not to tell you!" he exclaimed. "I wished
to surprise you. I have come home on a visit!"

Eleanor tried not to chuckle. She could guess what happened. The government field-trip boat must have put in at
the Puluwats bound eastward, and Nelson had somehow
gotten aboard. In a world where there were no seasons except for a change of winds, what significance had the calendar year and why have a set time for "making school?"

"And," Nelson added, with a little touch of the dramatic,
"I have brought someone with me!"

Eleanor stared. Coming up behind Nelson from among a
throng of islanders was a figure to arrest attention anywhere

on earth. It was the king of the nudist Puluwats! He was a
doughty little man, bare of chest, and upon his frame such
scant clothing as he wore hung with the air of having been
blown there by the wind. Plainly he had merely put it on
out of deference to his host. He walked with the grace of a
man who has moved all his life unhampered by clinging
garments. There was about him something of the legendary
"noble savage." Belt and suspenders were unknown to him,
yet somehow his shorts stayed in place and, wonder of wonders, a rakish black beret was cocked over one ear! Shades
of Montmartre and the Quartier Latin! Where had the
Puluwat king found that beret? And he wore it with an air!
A hat was no sillier to his mind than shirt or trousers and
a great deal less silly than buttons. His countenance radiated
absolute delight. Plainly he was having the time of his life,
living here on this high mountainous island, gazing at the
wonders of its forests and rivers. Rivers were unknown to
atoll dwellers. He had seen mountains on brief visits to
Truk, a vast atoll with high islands as well as outlying low
ones. When he returned to his own low island, he would be
counted a world-traveled man and could tell his people of
the wonderful trees and fruits he had seen, for on Kusaie,
limes, mountain apples, Kusaien oranges and breadfruit
grew in rich abundance.

Eleanor spoke to him in simple English. He answered
proudly with such words as he knew. It was amazing to
Eleanor how swiftly all the island people picked up a new
language. He could have had no teacher but Nelson, who
was a Kusaien.

"Are you pleased to have a missionary on your island?"
she asked the king.

"Very good! Very good!" The king's enthusiasm was too
genuine to be prompted by mere politeness. "Also Nelson's
son can count very good, very high. I need him very bad to
keep store."

Eleanor suspected that anything over the number of
fingers and toes might be baffling to many Puluwatese.

These people had been blasted out of their isolation only after the last war. Even the Japanese influence had not penetrated to their atoll as they had nothing to incite the cupidity of a conqueror. Plainly the new way of life met with the king's hearty approval.

"Everybody very happy!" he beamed. "Nelson, he taught us to smile, to sing. Once we did not know how!"

Eleanor knew this was literally true. Nelson had found only sullen faces on the Puluwats. He had taught them the joy of living and their almost instant response had been amazing.

She smiled at the king's wife and daughter, very properly clad in print dresses and Japanese zoris or sandals, these last being still standard trade goods in the islands. They stood shyly behind the king. She went over and shook hands with them. The fourteen-year-old daughter had married the son of the Kusaien missionary, so the royal clans of the two islands were united.

Nelson spoke with some pride. "I have translated some of our Kusaien hymns into their language for them. Now they can sing them very well!"

And forthwith the Puluwatese, joined by Nelson and his son, sang the old hymn tune in words that had never yet graced the pages of any book. Nelson had them written in pencil on a scrap of paper. He stood so the others could look over his shoulder. The king looked earnestly at the paper, his eyes round as an owl's, pretending to read from the mysterious scratches. Eleanor wondered if he could read or whether this was a little mark of sophistication he had chosen to assume. She reflected that the experiment of sending Nelson to the Puluwats had apparently been a huge success.

What individualists the islanders were! The islands seemed to bring out the personality both of their own people and of foreign sojourners. Perhaps it was because they lay so open to the sun. Privacy was impossible to achieve. Nothing was hidden, everything was known. Every object was in full sunlight or darkest shade. So with every facet of a human being. One was good or bad; a Christian or a non-Christian. It seemed impossible for anyone to choose a middle ground. This might well be the fundamental concept of island living that made the native Christians so unbending in their attitude toward any infractions of the church rules. They felt that if they once let down the bars, the line could not be held.

Certainly under the tropic sun, Eleanor's fellow Americans soon showed their true characters. Oddities in their natures, almost unnoticed at home, developed strongly. Weaknesses showed up with glaring clarity. Even the pious, early missionaries admitted noting in one another irritating characteristics when living under thatched roofs far from the amenities of civilization. Observing the number of outsiders who went to pieces in the islands, she concluded that it must be easier to behave with decorum in the shadow of Westminster Abbey than in the scanter shade of a coconut tree.

The days she could spend here in Kusaie slipped past like beads on a string. She could not visit all four villages but she saw as many of her friends as possible. This should not be her last visit to Kusaie in the natural course of things. She still had several tours of duty ahead, presumably in this area. But something made her visit every dear spot she could. Just in case, she told herself, just in case I never come back. She spent every minute she could with Queen Hattie, for her days appeared to be numbered.

"What kind of food could I send you from the *Star*?" Eleanor asked.

Hattie's eyes lighted. "I would like some coffee and catsup!"

Eleanor stifled a gasp. That *was* an odd combination. But perhaps she had acquired a taste for those two things when a child in the Gilberts. Presumably her father would have sent for some American food. Luckily, Eleanor had both items aboard the *Star* and was able to grant the Queen's wish.

They would not let their beloved missionary go away without a parting gift. King John had made for her a model of the bed of the ancient kings of Kusaie. So stringent was protocol that in former days not even the queen dared sleep on such a bed, on pain of death. Both missionary and anthropologist might puzzle over these oddities a lifetime and never come up with the reason for them.

Then there was the task of making the *Star* ready to go to sea. They must get aboard supplies of food, water and firewood. Lelet, being Marshallese, was growing restless for home, oppressed perhaps by the high mountains that were so strange to his eyes. He was like the old Nantucketer who made his first and only visit to the continent of North America at Cape Cod.

"How did you like it?" a neighbor asked.

The old fellow snorted indignantly. "Couldn't see it! It was all messed up with trees."

So Lelet no doubt missed consciously or otherwise the unbroken seascapes of his home.

Moreover, it was already June. He wished to be at Rong Rong Mission not later than June twentieth for the opening of the conference to be held there by the Association of Marshallese Churches, for Lelet was both pastor and mariner.

When the day came to leave, Eleanor's heart was leaden. She could not account for the mood and tried hard to shake it off. The shore was thronged with people. King John, Ernest, Nelson, the King of the Puluwats and his family. Even Palik and some of the pupils had come down from Mwot. Again there were generous gifts of food for the journey. When all were loaded aboard, there was scarcely room to stand on the schooner's deck.

It was the afternoon of June fourth. The sun was lowering and the mountains cast purple shadows on the ruffled

waters of the lagoon. The mountain tops were still in bright
sunshine. It was as if a kind of halo rested on the high peaks
of Kusaie. Eleanor looked back, locking this scene away in
her memory.

She pressed the hand of the old king as he said to her
with a confident smile, "We may not meet again here but I
will see you beyond the River!"

Then she stepped into the skiff to be rowed out to the
Star. The wind was wrong to leave the harbor. They could
not have made it under sail, but they had been offered a
tow. John Melander was waiting with his sturdy little motor
boat. Even against a headwind, he could take them out
through the pass. The motor caught and, as if by signal, the
people on shore began to sing. Everyone in the port of Lelu
joined in. Eleanor's eyes were moist. Among the voices
raised in the hymn she heard that of the old man who preferred the title of Pastor to that of King. She could hear
him long after the other voices had grown faint in the distance.

Then they were out of the pass. Palik, who had stayed on
the *Star* as long as possible, shook hands with Eleanor for
the last time, and leaped lightly into Melander's launch.
Luckabudge cast off the towline.

"Thank you, John!" Eleanor called gratefully. "We
should never have got out today without your help."

"Yokwe Kom!" the Marshallese Captain and crew yelled
after them.

John thrust his rudder hard over. "Good-bye, Mother
Wilson. Good-bye, boys. Come again! And come soon!"

Then with a put-putting of the motor, the small boat
circled, leaving a beautiful crescent-shaped wake on the
water. The *Star's* sails were already hoisted. Slowly they
filled. Lelet was at the wheel. They could still glimpse the
blur of white from the people standing on the shore, waving
with towels, shirts, and handkerchiefs.

Their course homeward to Majuro should have been 75
degrees, almost east by north, but the winds ruled otherwise.

A motor boat goes where she will, a sailboat where she can. She is the servant of the winds.

Lelet looked at the sea. Luckabudge studied the clouds. Eleanor bent a watchful eye on the compass. But there was only one way they could go with this wind, and that was almost due north. They would be lucky if they could make even five degrees to the east.

The Marshallese were elated. They had been on their argosy. They had seen the wonders of high islands. They were going home.

It was June twenty-second when, utterly exhausted, they sighted the tiny blue peaks that marked the long narrow reef of Majuro Atoll. To the uninitiated, these looked like miniature mountains. Island eyes knew them for what they were, clumps of tall coconut trees. The land was too low to be seen at this distance. Wind and tide were against them and they could not enter the pass that night. They beat back and forth waiting for morning when a favorable tide would take them in.

Eleanor was bone weary but she felt a strange exaltation. They had sailed from Majuro to Kwajalein, from Kwajalein to distant Ponape, and home by way of Mokil and Kusaie to Majuro again! Ulysses after ten years of wandering was no happier to see the peaks of craggy Ithaca, than she to see the reef of Majuro. No matter what happened she would never be a landlubber again.

This tour of duty was ended. Her leave was long past due and now the call of home, home in the States, was growing insistent. This time Eleanor would not delay her return. The school at Rong Rong had closed for the summer, but as always there were many things to attend to before she could leave. By sitting up most of the night, she was ready to leave on a ship sailing from Majuro to Kwajalein where she could catch a plane to Honolulu.

What was it she wanted so urgently? To see her home, her family, her dear ones? That came first, of course. But analyzing her emotions, she knew it was something else, not really important. She looked at her arms, burned by the tropic sun. Could she ever wash off the salt spray? She looked at her coral-cut shoes. She glanced at her faded, mended, bedraggled cotton dress. Who could keep clothes in any sort of order under all the difficulties of travel on a sailing vessel and through the rigors of life on a strip of sand? She glanced in the mirror. Under the rim of her pandanus hat, her hair hung in stray elf locks. She could wash it tonight and curl it after a fashion but she no longer dared trust an island barber to trim it. She did not want to go home looking like an Iroquois brave!

Then she knew quite suddenly what else she wanted. She wanted clean and lovely clothes that appeared magically out of paper bags fresh from the dry cleaner. She wanted proper shoes, not castoff navy boots or Japanese zoris, or old slippers cut and stained from island wear and mildewed in the climate of the equator. She wanted once again to have a permanent, to have her hair cut and shaped and styled in Boston, and she wanted to have it set regularly. She wanted most of all the feel of silk against her skin. And she was going to buy a bottle of fine perfume.

She looked about at her little Majuro house. Once it had seemed almost luxurious. Now it had shrunk to its true size. She wanted to live in a big house with a cellar under it—not a little house built on stilts set in the sand! She did not quite put it into words but what it came to was this: a New England lady, long away from home, wanted to get back for a little while into her own skin, into the manner of living to which she had been born.

Yet when the day came to go, she felt an odd mingling of emotions. She looked at the *Star*, riding at anchor off Rong Rong Mission. She was leaving it in the care of Loren Miller and his wife, the young couple that would live in her house and carry on her work while she was gone. And Luckabudge would be here. He had been promoted now to the rank of bo'sun. He would care for the *Star* as if it were his own.

Why then was she so troubled? She stood a moment on the beach looking back. A sharp pain pierced her. This was the fate of the man or woman who lived in two worlds. He must always suffer when he forsook one for the other. Perhaps David Livingston and the old-time missionaries had actually been better off. They buried themselves in darkest Africa or some other remote place and were cut off from the old world perhaps forever. They thrust down their roots once and for all in alien soil. At this moment she felt uprooted.

"Why am I going?" her heart asked. "Is not this my home? Are not these my people? Here I have carved out a little island world for myself! Do I really belong in Cambridge any more?"

Yet she had to find out. It was too late to back down now! The coast guard launch was waiting. And people had come to say good-bye. She was showered with gifts, even money for her journey, given by friends who could in no wise afford it. They were all lined up to shake hands with her. This was a custom never neglected in the islands.

With characteristic courtesy, the others stepped back, allowing Luckabudge to say the last farewell, since he had sailed with her so long, the only one of all the *Star's* company to carry through to the end. Luckabudge was not torn between two worlds as she was. He lived serenely in the only one he knew. Boston was to him a kind of spiritual homeland, rather like Heaven, which even though one could not see it, was surely there. It was the place from which good, generous people had sent to his island ships, Bibles, and missionaries because they cared for men's immortal souls.

They stood together—Eleanor and Luckabudge, two old shipmates about to be parted for a little. Their eyes turned toward their ship riding at her mooring in the lagoon. She was getting old but there was something gallant, something undaunted about the way she rode the swell, rising and falling, straining at her ropes. She was not finished yet, not yet!

Luckabudge looked at Eleanor. To her that look seemed a kind of benediction. His eyes were moist.

"Mother Wilson," he said gently, "come safe to your home and to your dear brother's house. And remember me to your family, to the church people—to everyone you meet!"